Photographing Birds
Art and Techniques

Photographing Birds
Art and Techniques

Mark Sisson

CROWOOD

First published in 2014 by
The Crowood Press Ltd
Ramsbury, Marlborough
Wiltshire SN8 2HR

www.crowood.com

British Library Cataloguing-in-Publication Data
A catalogue record for this book is available from the British Library.

ISBN 978 1 84797 713 7

Frontispiece: Mute Swan cygnet *Cygnus olor*.

Acknowledgements

Bird photography, like all aspects of nature photography, is generally a very solitary profession. In spite of this there are a number of people who have helped both in terms of career in this field and the love of the natural world that took me down this path in the first place. Firstly my family: my wife Caroline, our children and my parents have all had to put up with my long absences and at times obsessive nature in pursuit of my work, but all have been hugely supportive in the process. Professionally speaking my Natures Images colleagues Danny Green, Paul Hobson and Edwin Kats have been among the many photographers who have inspired and aided my learning in this field: a process that never ends. Finally the many organizations I have had and still enjoy the pleasure of working for, including Shropshire Wildlife Trust and the RSPB to name only a couple: you all do great conservation work and I hope my images are of genuine help and use in your causes.

Graphic design and layout by www.peggyandco.ca
Printed and bound in Singapore by Craft Print International

CONTENTS

Introduction

There are many routes into the world of bird photography. For some it is a natural and these days reasonably affordable addition to the record-keeping that many keen ornithologists undertake. For those starting from a photographic knowledge base, it offers the excitement of one of the most challenging genres of photography there is, and certainly one that at times tests even modern high-specification cameras to their limits. For many, however, it is part of a desire to experience, enjoy and interpret an integral part of the natural world, and probably the most visible, varied and accessible to them in terms of subject, wherever they may live.

Whether or not any or even all of these apply to you, there is no doubt that bird photography is a pastime that has increased dramatically in recent years with the emergence of high-specification and in real terms significantly more affordable digital SLR cameras and incredibly fast-focusing long lenses. The days of expensive processing of slides taken using a split-prism manually pre-focused wind-on camera are now well and truly gone. There is also a plethora of individuals and companies offering photographic experience days, short-breaks and longer adventures focused on bird photography, so the accessibility of stunning subject material is now just a swipe of a credit card away! You only have to spend a short while surfing the internet to come across image after colourful image of birds in all manner of locations and with ever-increasing standards of creativity in their capture, so if this really is your area of interest then it's as good a time to start as any.

All of that said, there is still, as in so many aspects of life, no better way to approach things than by really understanding your subject, really understanding your working tools and then looking to develop your own style and approach, and you should find some solid building blocks and pointers towards this in this book. The one thing the book won't be able to teach you, though – and probably the greatest attribute any photographer of any aspect of the natural world can have – is patience. Our modern lifestyles make it all too easy to change channels if we're bored and constantly keep in touch with friends or colleagues on whatever portable device we happen to have this year. While many of these technologies can help the process of bird photography, they simply cannot replace the need for patience, observation and time spent watching, learning and interpreting the behaviour of your photographic subject. Alongside technical, creative and practical insights these pages therefore look to offer the beginner and enthusiast some pointers to not simply achieving a more consistent and better standard of image, but also developing the mindset and outlook that will help them do so.

◀ Fig. 0.1
Red-necked Phalarope *Phalaropus lobatus* wading in the shallows of Lake Myvatn, Iceland. Canon 1Dx, 500mm + 1.4× converter, ƒ5.6, 1/4000sec, ISO 800.

Chapter 1

Equipment

CHOOSING A DIGITAL SLR

If this book had been written even just ten years ago the decision-making process when it comes to camera selection would have been far more complicated than it is today. Digital cameras in their various guises were relatively new on the market and in terms of final image quality simply didn't match up to a well-taken slide or transparency.

Today it's almost impossible to find anyone working seriously in the field of wildlife photography who doesn't rely exclusively on a digital camera and this will almost definitely be an SLR (single lens reflex) camera – a system which allows interchangeable lenses to be added to a camera body, the viewfinder of which provides a view which looks directly through the lens thanks to a mechanical mirror and pentaprism inside. When the shutter is pressed to take an image the mirror swings out of the way, allowing the lens to project light through the aperture onto a digital sensor at the rear of the camera, a process that generally takes a fraction of a second. Although the zoom (or magnification) capabilities of many so-called bridge cameras are indeed quite significant, and there are even now mirrorless interchangeable lens camera systems, these styles of cameras do have limitations in terms of the amount and degree of control you can really have over them. They also very often have a significant delay between pressing the shutter and taking the image

▲ Fig. 1.2
A modern, professional-specification digital SLR.

that will soon have you wishing you had spent that bit more on an SLR in the first place.

It is not the author's place to advise on a specific brand or model of SLR, but in making that choice for yourself it makes sense to be guided by a number of pointers, such as the breadth of camera bodies and lenses that the manufacturer has to offer – a good indication of their range and a quick bit of researching on what kit the photographers you might aspire to image-wise are using can be a good starting point. It generally comes down to a couple of choices, either of which will see you right. Beyond making a decision as to whether a full-frame or crop-sensor body is your best bet (*see* box), it is then a question of budget. Camera bodies are a bit like new cars: there is an array of price-points, all of which depreciate almost immediately as new

◀ Fig. 1.1
Black-winged Stilt *Himantopus himantopus* in the wetland area of Hortobagy National Park, Hungary. Canon 1Dx, 500mm +1.4× converter, ƒ5.6, 1/2000sec, ISO 1600.

models are constantly being brought out. The best advice is to aspire to one at the top end of your budget, work it hard for a number of years, and you will know when you have out-grown it and can justify (as well as afford) trading up. You will also know by then which features have proved to be a touch more frustrating than ideal and can research them specifically at that next stage, too.

Read plenty of reviews and look particularly at the camera's speed and accuracy of focusing and frames-per-second capabilities (a minimum of five per second is necessary). These are the capabilities that will be most tested by bird photography as a genre. It is also important to try the camera out ergonomically – there can be quite a bit of variety in terms of size and it needs to fit comfortably in your hands.

CHOOSING LENSES

The reality of bird photography is that if you really want to take it seriously you are going to need a reasonably long telephoto lens and these do come with a high price tag. Our view of the world using our eyes is roughly the equivalent to looking through a 50mm lens on a full-frame sensor camera. Anything greater than 50mm is moving into telephoto territory. For most bird photography the simple fact of the matter is that you will have to be working at a reasonable distance from your subject, and as many bird species are small in size a long telephoto lens is essential. 300mm is probably the absolute minimum and the norm that you will see most professionals using is a 500mm.

FULL-FRAME VERSUS CROP SENSOR

Full-frame digital SLRs have had their sensors (the area where the image data is recorded) sized to match the old 35mm film format – namely 36mm × 24mm. These large sensors are generally more expensive than crop- (or APS-C) sized sensors and are therefore more likely to be found in high specification models. There are, though, advantages and disadvantages when it comes to bird photography. On the plus side they have large photosites (the light-sensitive points on the chip), which means they are able to capture more light with less noise, resulting in a less grainy and smoother image; this also means they are generally able to work better in low light conditions. A fast shutter speed is often important in bird photography so this can be a major help towards this.

Crop sensor SLRs (most consumer-level models fall into this bracket) have an APS-C size chip. Depending on the manufacturer, this means a sensor ranging from 20.7mm × 13.8mm to 28.7mm × 19.1mm. The main impact of this is the apparent multiplication of the focal length of the lens attached to the camera – hence why these are often referred to as 1.3× or 1.6× crop. This makes a 300mm lens the equivalent of a 390mm or 480mm lens respectively. Using these bodies the equivalent focal length of longer (and more expensive) lenses can be achieved more economically, and subjects that won't tolerate being approached too closely can still be photographed from a greater distance.

▲ Fig. 1.3
A 300mm lens (shown here with a protective neoprene coating) is very much the minimum focal length required for professional and high-end bird photography.

▲ Fig. 1.4
A 1.4x tele-converter adds an additional 40 per cent magnification to your lens, turning a 500mm lens into 700mm: you do lose a stop of light, though.

Budgets will always be a factor here, but as with your selection of camera body my advice is to spend at the top end of your budget. A good lens will last through several changes of camera body, and in this field the simple rule that you pay for what you get applies – higher quality glass simply does give cleaner and sharper images. Although they don't appear very often, looking on internet auction sites for secondhand lenses can prove fruitful and is an additional reassurance that you should have little problem recouping much, if not all, of your outlay should your circumstances change.

Another factor to bear in mind other than the quality/budget equation is the weight of the lens and camera combination. Although most of the time you will be using a tripod (*see* 'Supporting your Camera', below) or some other form of support, you still have to be able to comfortably lift and manoeuvre your kit, as well as carry it to photographic locations away from home. Before investing in this area make sure you get to feel the weight of your potential purchase by visiting a retail outlet or an exhibition where the equipment may be on display.

Working with these long lenses does mean that fast shutter speeds are preferable in order to avoid the dreaded 'camera shake' in your images. Many manufacturers have additional image stabilization or vibration reduction technologies built into their lenses, and although they add to the cost they are extremely beneficial and another factor to consider in your decision-making.

Alongside your long lens, a wide-angle lens (24–70mm for example) will prove a useful addition. This style of lens will significantly exaggerate the perspective of your images – put simply, objects close to the camera will appear larger than they are and those in the distance seem further away. Although this lens type is the bread-and-butter for landscape photographers, it has a role in creating images that emphasize the context of the habitat your subject may be in. This may require the use of remote shutter release, as relatively few wild subjects will come that close.

PRIME LENS VERSUS ZOOM

Lenses come in essentially two different types. Prime lenses are those of a fixed focal length (for example, 300mm) and this cannot be changed. Zoom lenses offer a range of adjustable focal lengths that the user can easily adjust during use (for example, 70–200mm). While the advantages of the latter are indeed many, offering as they do a wider range of compositional options and often a significantly cheaper route to achieving the longer focal lengths you may be seeking, prime lenses do tend to be much sharper from an optical perspective, and are generally much 'faster', offering wider minimum apertures such as $f2.8$ or $f4$, which means they can be used more easily in lower light conditions.

▲ Fig. 1.5
A 24–70mm is an ideal wide-angle lens (shown here with lens hood).

▼ Fig. 1.6
This confiding Atlantic Puffin *Fratercula arctica,* photographed in the dramatic setting of the cliffs at Hermaness in Shetland at a focal length of 50mm, shows just how the context of the bird's habitat can add to the drama of an image.

SUPPORTING YOUR CAMERA

Having already highlighted the need for a long telephoto lens for most bird photography work and the associated issues of weight that come with it, making sure that your camera and lens are well supported is another essential ingredient. Key here is a good, solid tripod with a flexible head on it, to which the camera and lens are attached.

Tripods

As in almost everything in this equipment chapter, setting yourself a budget and then looking to invest towards the top-end of it will always pay off in the longer term. Buy a cheap and flimsy tripod (usually these come with the head and legs combined) and you almost may as well not bother as it really won't help; in fact it will probably hinder your photography, such will be the frustration it will engender.

There are a number of leading tripod manufacturers to choose from, all of whom offer the same essential design. Key things to look out for are strong and adjustable legs (if this is provided in a lightweight material such as carbon fibre so much the better, as it will reduce the burden of gear-carrying), ideally a maximum height that means if you are photographing from a standing position you can minimize the bending of your back to look through the camera, and personally I would avoid a centre column so that when you open the legs out to get the tripod as close to the ground as possible it goes almost flat. If you do get a model with a centre column, make sure it is removable.

▲ Fig. 1.7
This tripod is very solid yet reasonably lightweight thanks to its carbon fibre legs, which can be extended to full standing height if required or opened flat for photographing at ground level: note the absence of a centre column to make this easier.

Tripod Heads

On top of this you will require a tripod head that provides the attachment to the camera and lens combination. The three main design options are a ball head (akin to a ball and socket joint), a pan and tilt head, and a bracket design.

The former allows the camera to rotate while it's attached to the ball itself and be locked into position. Although they are highly flexible they can be quite fiddly to lock into position at speed and are possibly therefore more suited to landscape photography. Pan and tilt heads allow movement left to right, forwards and backwards, as well as horizontal panning. They provide excellent and often very

▲ Fig. 1.8a
A ball head: its movement is similar to a ball and socket joint.

▲ Fig. 1.8b
A pan and tilt head.

▲ Fig. 1.8c
A gimbal-style head based on a bracket design offers the greatest flexibility with long lenses. If your budget will run to it, it is the best option for bird photography once you have invested in the longer lens.

precise support but can be quite bulky and heavy design-wise and, like the ball heads, can be quite awkward with longer lenses. The third option of a bracket design or gimbal-style head is really designed with the long lenses of bird photography in mind. The camera and lens combination is balanced at its natural centre of gravity around a central point of rotation and the resultant effort required to move the direction the lens points is minimal. They are an expensive option without doubt, but for long and heavy lenses they are certainly the most flexible and easy-to-use option. It is important to note, though, that you will require an additional lens plate on the foot of your telephoto lens in order to attach everything together and this will need to be purchased separately.

Other Supports

Many sports photographers, also users of long lenses, use a monopod as their preferred method of support, citing flexibility, a lighter weight and greater manoeuvrability as the reason. In essence it is a single-legged tripod; the better ones have adjustable leg sections (again, check the maximum height) and some offer options as to how the foot end can be secured to the ground (a spike for instance). They can be a useful option when stalking and also on small boats where space is restricted and constant motion renders a tripod almost useless.

▲ Fig. 1.9
This image of a male King Eider *Somateria spectabilis* was photographed using a 500mm lens while travelling at reasonable speed in a zodiac-style rib boat in northern Norway. Tripods were not possible for support but a monopod wedged into the floor of the boat helped significantly in comparison to straightforward hand-holding.

A beanbag is also an excellent form of support and highly flexible. For the filling, rice or dried peas are generally a little more eco-friendly that polystyrene balls (some of which always blow away when you empty or refill) and their pliant nature allows the bag to form nicely around a long lens when placed somewhere stable as a base. These are particularly useful when working out of a car window (especially those that come in an 'H'-type shape as they fit over the door well when the window is down) or in hides where there is a suitable shelf in front of the opening. They also work well when you have to set up in a prone position on the ground in a bag hide and a tripod is too bulky.

▲ Fig. 1.10
A beanbag, whether a commercially bought one (as here) or home-made and filled with rice or pulses, provides excellent moulding-type support for long lenses when tripods are not possible.

Finally, the one bit of support that comes with your camera when you buy it is a neck strap. When you are using long lenses and tripods these are by and large irrelevant to the carrying of your camera and frankly get in the way, so it's generally best not to bother attaching them to the camera body.

USEFUL ACCESSORIES

There is an almost endless range of accessories marketed at photographers, many of which are of limited long-term usefulness, but the following suggestions are useful additions to consider as you become more committed to your hobby.

Spare Batteries/Battery Grip

Top-end SLRs come with large battery packs which contain a number of individual battery cells inside. Under most circumstances these will happily last out a day's photography but it is always good practice to have a spare or two in your kit bag, especially when photographing away from home. Entry-level SLRs have much smaller battery packs and these run out much quicker, making this more essential. It is possible to get a vertical battery grip for these, which attaches via the camera's battery storage compartment. This will not only provide increased storage space by allowing for the use of two batteries, but also provide an additional shutter-release button, making using it in portrait-format images infinitely easier.

Angle Finder

When your camera is pressed flat to the ground with you lying behind it, contorting your neck to look through the viewfinder can sometimes be impossible. The same issues apply (albeit with different consequences) should you be set up at water level with your tripod in the water! In both of these instances a right-angle viewfinder is an excellent solution. It slots onto your viewfinder like a ninety-degree periscope, allowing easy visibility. It does take a bit of mental re-orientation when it comes to seeing and composing your images (especially getting level horizons), so practise a bit before a first serious outing.

▲ Fig. 1.11
This additional battery grip will house not only two batteries (it slots into the existing battery compartment of the camera) but also a new set of shutter-release and general control buttons for use when shooting in portrait mode.

▲ Fig. 1.12
Working with a 90-degree angle finder will allow you to get the camera even lower to the ground or water and still be able to look through the viewfinder to compose and focus your images.

Filters

Long telephoto lenses don't lend themselves easily to the addition of filters, but some do have a slot for drop-in versions. As a result filters generally are of less use for bird photography than in most other areas of outdoor photography. A polarizing filter, though, which reduces glare (especially on water) and also increases the intensity and saturation of colours (especially blue skies) in much the same way as a pair of sunglasses does, is a good addition to the kit bag for using on a wide-angle lens, especially as the habitat itself will be key to any images taken.

◀ Fig. 1.13
A polarizing filter will really help to intensify colour and saturation in your images. This is a slot-in square version from Lee, but there are screw-in filters that will attach directly to your lens as well; you need to rotate the filter to get the maximum polarization effect from it.

▲ Fig. 1.14
Although this image of a Common Buzzard *Buteo buteo* was taken under controlled conditions, the use of a polarizing filter to give some additional punch to the clouds and sky in particular has added an extra element in terms of its impact.

Flashgun

Entry-level SLR cameras generally come with a pop-up flash, but many more advanced models don't, so if you want to use artificial lighting a flashgun becomes a necessity. Whether you will wish to do so will be very much a matter of personal choice and style. Flashguns are quite cumbersome and awkward to use, often have quite short distance reach without the purchase of additional accessories, and even when used very carefully to minimize their visual impact there is a certain uniformity about the images created when using them. Their use will be covered in Chapter 3. If purchasing one, stick with the manufacturer's brand that matches your camera and look for as high a Guide Number as you can afford, as they reflect the power output (and therefore distance coverage) of the unit.

▲ Fig. 1.15
This flashgun is attached conventionally to the camera body, but can equally be taken off the body with a wired connection or fired on a remote basis using wireless triggers. The diffuser over the flash itself helps to diffuse the light, making it more even.

LOOKING AFTER YOUR GEAR

Photographic equipment does not come cheaply, and if you get seriously into bird photography the chances are that you will have some very expensive items that you will be using, carrying and occasionally having to transport overseas, so they do need looking after with the appropriate care and attention. Add in the fact that many of the locations you may be working in offer some environmental challenges at times and it becomes even more necessary. Underpinning this day-to-day care, it is important to make sure that your camera equipment is properly insured. It may be that your household contents insurance will do this, but the chances are that every lens, camera body and possibly even tripod/tripod head combination will need listing as a named item; check your policy carefully. You will also need to check just what the level and nature of cover for your equipment is when using it away from home and how this applies to travel, especially overseas. You will also need to check whether the circumstances of this general policy change should you start to make any form of commercial return out of your images. If this is the case (and if your equipment list starts to reach a significant figure you may want to consider this regardless), then looking for specialist photographic equipment/photographer insurance policies is very much recommended. The author has had to make claims against his more than once and has been very grateful that he had a good policy in place on each occasion!

▲ Fig. 1.16
However well designed and spacious, any backpack will always become full to the brim: the battle between keeping weight to a minimum and yet having everything you may need to hand is never won.

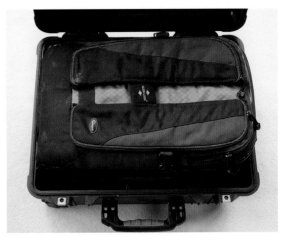

▲ Fig. 1.17
This extremely hard Peli case is the right size to allow your backpack (and all its additional padding) to fit straight in it if you need extra protection when your kit is in transit. You can alternatively buy a foam insert to the case and place the individual items in gaps you cut out.

Backpack

A good rucksack-style backpack is almost certainly the most comfortable and practical way of storing and carrying your gear. There will almost always be a walk of some sort to your location, occasionally very long if you are working with species like Ptarmigan who live on the mountaintops, so it's important that whatever your storage it is comfortable to carry. Backpacks tend to be more spacious and easy on the shoulders than the older-style shoulder bags.

There are many brands, shapes and sizes but you need to consider the array of equipment that you are likely to have on any one excursion and be sure that it will all fit – the length of your longest lens is usually the determining factor. Check that the zips open easily (and quietly) to allow quick access to your kit, and if you can find an option that allows your main body and lens to be connected up rather than separated you will be ready to shoot much quicker should you come across something unexpected that you want to photograph.

A further consideration comes when looking to travel internationally and wanting to take your kit on a plane. Placing equipment of this value routinely into the hold is not recommended, so ensuring your backpack is the correct size to be taken onboard as your carry-on item is an essential element in your final choice of design. On the occasions where strict weight allowances prevent this (although careful selection of airlines will generally avoid this – many have no weight restrictions on carry-on bags or surprisingly high ones anyway when compared to others), the use of a hard and lockable case (Peli are the main manufacturers of these) into which your backpack can be placed to ensure full padding/protection is recommended.

Rain Sleeve/Dust Cover

Since bird photography is an outdoor occupation, the chances of undertaking it during inclement weather are high, especially in the UK. In fact deliberately heading out to photograph in difficult weather conditions is recommended, as the resulting images can be very impactful. This makes it especially important to ensure that your camera and lens are suitably protected.

As a starter it is good practice to have a neoprene cover of some sort – as a coat, if you like – on your long lens on a permanent basis. These provide some protection against day-to-day scratches, light drizzle and also some camouflage, especially necessary if you have a bright white lens in the first place! When the rain starts, a reversible dust/rain cover that fits over the lens and camera body combined, while still allowing you to carry on working, is essential; a simple plastic bag will only suffice in a really light, short shower. Again, these come in various camouflage types and are available from companies such as Wildlife Watching Supplies to fit whatever lens/camera combination you have. When working in dry, dusty climates or on a windswept beach, it is equally important to use the cover – dust is as much if not more of a potential hazard to your kit as rain.

Sensor Cleaning

Although cameras are now designed to automatically 'clean' your sensor every time you switch them off, there is still every chance that if you are working in a dry or sandy location you will get the occasional dust spot on your sensor. Remembering to turn your camera off when you change lenses will help here, as the sensor is more magnetically charged and attractive to dust when it is switched on. If it does happen and it is just a small piece of dust, don't be tempted to use a cloth or your finger to remove it – instead give it a gentle brush using, for instance, the Arctic Butterfly sensor brush (this battery-operated brush has an attractive charge in its filaments to

▲ Fig. 1.18
The neoprene coating shown on this 300mm lens provides not only camouflage (essential when protruding from a hide) but also protection against inevitable scratches and the weather conditions you are likely to take it out in.

▲ Fig. 1.19
This reversible rain and dust cover will add a further protective layer to your camera and lens in pretty much most conditions that you would be out photographing in.

▲ Fig. 1.20
This Arctic Butterfly brush is ideal for removing small dust particles from your sensor.

help pull any dust off your sensor), a small and light piece of kit to help you out both in the field and back at home. If the offending article is more stubborn, you will need to take the body to a dealer for a more thorough sensor clean.

Image Storage in the Field

The images you capture are recorded on the storage cards in your camera and these too need protecting and looking after sensibly – no insurance cover can replace them! Some cameras offer a choice of card types to work with, and if the opportunity to use the more solid and robust compact flash cards is there then these are recommended. The storage capacity of these cards is now huge (64GB) and they are increasingly affordable, but rather than risk having all your images on one card that may get lost, damaged or corrupted, however carefully you look after it, using several smaller storage cards (say 16GB) is probably better practice. Keeping a selection of pre-formatted versions of these in a hard-cased storage wallet (and generally in a coat pocket for speedy access), and storing ready-to-use cards one way up and used ones another, will mean you can change to a new card quickly when necessary while keeping them safe.

Portable storage devices or viewers are another way of backing up your cards, but unless you are away from power for a number of days then a good selection of storage cards is generally more cost- and space-effective. You can transfer the images to a laptop/net book as well as an additional freestanding hard drive back at base overnight before reformatting them for use the next day.

▲ **Fig. 1.21**
A hard-cased compact flash card holder with a selection of cards. Note the one turned back to front – a simple way of identifying which are ready to use and which are full of images, something that can save time when changing to a new card in a hurry.

▲ **Fig. 1.22**
This hard and durable portable hard drive is an ideal way to back up images through your laptop while on a trip.

Chapter 2

Understanding Your SLR Camera

FILE FORMATS: JPEG, TIFF, RAW

Whether in-camera or during the post-processing phase of file management, you will encounter a number of different types of image file. And on most SLR cameras you can also choose the type of file you take your images in when you capture them. It is therefore important to understand the differences between them.

JPEG

JPEG is actually an acronym that stands for Joint Photographic Experts Group, who developed the file compression method that this file type uses. In essence, this is a file that is squashed so that it takes up a significantly reduced amount of storage space. Although this is good news in terms of space on cards and hard drives, it does have some disadvantages in that the process of compressing the file means that some of the original information in it is lost. This is not really noticeable to the human eye, but the more dramatic a series of changes or adjustments you make to a JPEG and the more times you re-save it in the process then the more the quality of the file breaks down. It is also a file format that the camera will have made some adjustments to in order to produce. These are parameters that you can set via the camera's menu and include elements such as white balance, saturation and sharpening. It is also a file format that is pretty much universally viewable and transferable on PC, Mac, tablet and phone.

TIFF

This too is an acronym, standing for Tagged Image File Format. Some early digital cameras used to allow you to capture your images as TIFF files, but since they are uncompressed files they take up significantly more space on your storage card, and they were very slow to write from camera to card so would regularly lock the camera's buffer up (the buffer is the storage capacity used for transferring image data to the card). Like JPEGs they are a format that can be easily read across viewing platforms and being uncompressed they retain the maximum amount of detail and information possible. They are therefore an ideal format for keeping your final images in post-processing and are the format most routinely required by image libraries and publications.

RAW

This file format is pretty much exactly as it describes itself – an unadulterated and unprocessed file taken straight from the camera sensor. Conceptually at least it is the equivalent of the negative/positive of film or slide in pre-digital days. The parameters that are applied by the camera to JPEGs are merely recorded in the metadata of a RAW file, which means that it needs to undergo a further stage of processing once it has been downloaded onto your computer in order to either go with these parameters or make a series of adjustments to them before producing a TIFF or JPEG. The biggest advantage of this is that the final output will have the look and feel you want, allowing you to have far greater control over the subtleties of the process itself. Even in the last few

◀ Fig. 2.1
Herring Gull *Larus argentatus* in full cry and summer plumage in Wexford, Ireland. Canon 1D Mk4, 500mm, ƒ5.6, 1/2000sec, ISO 400.

years the quality of software for processing RAW files has improved significantly and this allows you to revisit old files and reprocess them again for even better results, something that cannot be considered with JPEGs.

One of the questions I am regularly asked is which of these file formats to use. The simple answer to this is that, once you are comfortable with the post-processing side of things (*see* Chapter 9), working with RAW files when taking your pictures gives you far greater control and flexibility over the final look and feel of your images when it comes to processing them, even allowing you to pretty easily recover slight under or overexposure issues. Working with RAW files does introduce an initial step to the processing work (and possibly an additional software requirement as well) but with a good understanding of this most images can be processed within a minute or so. Until you are comfortable with the processing side of things, though, starting out using JPEG as a file format, but ensuring you have the largest and finest file size and quality your camera will allow is the most sensible place to begin. Making sure you get your exposure right at the point of taking the image does become more critical, but this is a good way to learn and something that you should be striving for in any case.

WHITE BALANCE

The white balance settings on your camera are its way of compensating for the changeable shades of colour (or colour casts) that different light sources and their associated colour temperatures create. These temperatures are measured in Kelvin and typically range from about 3000K at sunset through to 7000K in deep shade. Often we don't perceive these differences with our eyes as our brain does the equivalent job for us, and this makes white balance a potentially complex area to get to grips with.

▲ Figs 2.2a, 2.2b and 2.2c
This trio of images of a Robin *Erithacus rubecula* are in fact the same in all bar the white balance, which has been adjusted in this case in post-processing. **(a)** represents a normal daylight Kelvin reading of around 5400, **(b)** has warmed the image considerably to around 6200 (a cloudy setting), and **(c)** has cooled it to around 4200.

A simple way to think of it is to imagine you are photographing a piece of white paper. Photograph it in normal midday sunlight and it does appear white, but do so once the sky fills with cloud and it will take

▲ Fig. 2.3
This image of a Puffin displaying was taken approaching 11:15 at
night (albeit in the Shetland Isles in mid-July), but using a high
ISO meant that image-taking was still possible.

on a bluish tone, and in the early or late light of the
day an orange one, and all the while to our eyes it
will appear white in the first place!

The camera needs to be able to compensate for
these subtle and to us unnoticeable colour shifts,
and this is the role of white balance. In cloudy
conditions it will warm the image up, and in warm
evening light it will cool it down – always looking
to achieve something approaching a neutral look
and feel. Most cameras will have a series of icons to
help with this – a cloud for cloudy conditions, as an
example.

Leaving the camera set to Auto White Balance
is of course a solution here, especially if you are
shooting RAW files where you have the chance to
alter it during the initial processing stage, but trying

to achieve an image as close to the final result at the
point of capture is generally a sound approach, so
being prepared to be flexible and think about white
balance options while you are photographing is
recommended.

UNDERSTANDING ISO

In pre-digital days when you bought your film there
was an ISO number on the side, which was known
as the film speed. If you were heading to warm
sunny climes for your holidays a rating of 100 was
generally recommended, but if staying at home
in the more cloudy UK 400 was more likely to be

required. This was because with high ISO values you were able to take pictures in duller conditions as the film required less light to capture the image.

The same principle applies to the digital sensor in your camera, but now it is changeable from image to image at the click of a proverbial switch, so is a hugely valuable solution to challenging light conditions. Early digital cameras were prone to significant issues in terms of digital noise (not precisely the same as the graininess of high ISO films but with the same end result of degraded picture quality), especially once you ventured into territories over a setting of 400 or so.

High ISO noise improvement has been one of the main focus areas in the development of SLRs in recent years, and high-end SLRs with an ISO range from 100 to 12000+ produce extremely acceptable results, even at the top end of this range. Given that every step up in ISO gives an increase in either shutter speed or aperture (*see below*), this equates to a really useful 'Get Out Of Jail' card when it comes to photographing in poor light, such as in a wood or forest or in the early and later parts of the day.

APERTURES AND SHUTTER SPEEDS

For many people, acquiring an understanding of shutter speeds and apertures (the latter being the dreaded *f*-stop) is the hardest part of getting to a position of control of their SLR camera. To be fair, modern cameras are extremely good when left on an auto setting, but if you want to take your photography seriously you should apply some creativity to what you are doing. Quite simply, to be in control of the process you need to understand exactly what is going on with regard to these two elements that go to make up the correct exposure of your image.

One way to consider the basic principles is to recollect the pinhole cameras you at some point probably drew in your science lessons at school. The aperture is simply the size of the hole through which the light passes on its way to the digital sensor at the back of the camera; the shutter speed is the amount of time that it is open for.

The aperture is measured by the *f*-stop and, depending on the lens this can range from a very wide aperture (which lets a lot of light through) such as *f*2.8 or *f*4 to a very small aperture (which lets very little light through) such as *f*32. Each step-change in value either halves or doubles the amount of light let through.

The aperture you choose has a critical role in determining just how much of the image is in focus – the elements that are sharp as opposed to blurred. A wide aperture (e.g. *f*2.8) has a very small depth of field, whereas a narrow aperture (e.g. *f*22) has a much greater one. This will therefore have a huge impact on the look and feel of your final image. Most bird photography is of necessity taken with reasonably wide apertures and this helps ensure an out-of-focus background – a canvas of colour, if you like – on which your subject is captured.

The shutter speed, or amount of time the shutter is open for, is generally measured in fractions of a second, although most SLRs will have a range from anything as long as 1/30sec through to 1/4000sec – an extraordinarily short fraction of time when you stop and consider it. Adjustments to shutter speed works in precisely the same way as the aperture in that each full stop change either doubles or halves the amount of light passing through the camera. Given that most birds as subjects are likely to be active, a reasonably fast shutter speed is something you should generally be looking to aim for. As a rough guide, matching the focal length of your lens is not a bad starting point (i.e. for a 300mm lens a shutter speed of 1/300sec or faster). Once you start working on birds in flight, then the faster the better; slow shutter speeds, too, have a role when it comes to more creative interpretations.

◄ Figs 2.4a and 2.4b
These images of a Great Skua *Stercorarius skua* were taken of the same bird in the same location in Iceland, both using the same 500mm lens. In the first the aperture is wide open (ƒ4) and as a result there is little definition in the background – a smooth, de-focused effect. In the second more consideration was given to including some recognition of place in the background, so an aperture of ƒ11 was required to achieve it.

The final concept to understand is that there is no one correct combination of aperture and shutter speed for any given set of light conditions – 1/125sec at ƒ8 will give the same overall exposure as 1/500sec at ƒ4. What will change, though, is the depth of field and also the sharpness of any movement occurring in the image.

EXPOSURE AND GETTING IT RIGHT

Never think 'I'll fix that in Photoshop later', particularly if you believe the exposure of the image is wrong. Firstly there is always degradation in quality if you try to significantly change the exposure of an image in your post-processing, but more importantly the information available to you as you shoot, in particular the histogram on your camera (*see* box), tells you if you are getting it right or whether you need to make a simple adjustment or improvement. Put simply, there is no reason to get exposure significantly wrong.

SHOOTING MODES

Your camera will have (along with its many icon-driven modes which are largely irrelevant) essentially three potential shooting modes to operate it:

Manual

In this mode you select the aperture and shutter speed settings independently.

Aperture priority

In this mode you select the aperture and the camera calculates the shutter speed.

Shutter speed priority

In this mode you select the shutter speed and the camera calculates the aperture.

In the latter two of these modes you can apply some compensation to the part of the equation the camera is calculating, using exposure compensation adjustment. In other words if the camera is underexposing the image (i.e. the histogram is too far to the left), some positive compensation will correct this when you re-take the image and will move the histogram to the right, but most importantly it will only change the element of the equation you have considered is not the priority, thereby retaining the aperture you have chosen if, for instance, you are using aperture priority mode.

Which of the modes you choose will depend on what you consider to be the most important aspect of the image you are trying to capture – if it is depth of field it will be aperture priority, or if

it is how movement is captured it will be shutter speed priority. Remember, though, that shooting in aperture priority mode at the widest aperture will by default give you the fastest shutter speed that the light conditions (or ISO you have chosen) will allow, making this a good general starting point for most bird photography.

METERING MODES

In order to calculate the correct exposure combination it is necessary to take a light meter reading off the subject your camera is pointing at. Most SLR cameras come with three different metering modes – matrix, centre-weighted and spot metering.

The first of these, matrix, is the most sophisticated as it takes information from all over the scene through your lens to give a reading that is a weighted average, using its programmed algorithms. Centre-weighted biases this significantly to a pre-defined area in the centre of the frame, and the more precise spot metering takes a reading from whichever focal point you select and the scene/tonal range directly behind it.

In the days of film, spot metering was the most accurate way to meter – looking for a mid-tone to meter off ensured a well-balanced exposure. This principle still applies with digital SLRs but the ability to leave your viewing screen set up to immediately show the histogram of the first image (or test image) you take allows a speedier process using matrix metering and a quick adjustment of the exposure compensation to move the histogram as required. Shooting in aperture priority mode, this compensation adjustment will fool the camera into recalculating the associated shutter speed, thereby ensuring your required aperture is maintained and a good exposure still achieved. This methodology places great emphasis on understanding and interpreting the histogram, but since this is the one piece of

UNDERSTANDING THE HISTOGRAM

In some respects the histogram is the key piece of information that your digital SLR is able to show you once you have taken an image. Even though the quality of screens on the back of cameras is improving all the time, they are still so small that you are seeing just a fraction of the pixels that make up the image, so being absolutely sure everything is sharp and straight really has to be left until the image is on the computer in the processing phase. They are also very unreliable when it comes to being sure that the exposure you have is right or not – especially as a tweak of the brightness slider can make a dull image look great. Bright sunshine on the screen can be a hindrance in checking this way, too.

The histogram, however, gives an immediate clue as to what your exposure really consists of and it makes every sense to have this quick-check graph set up for instant review alongside your image on your camera.

Reading the histogram is quite straightforward. It is in essence a bar chart, where all the pure black pixels in your image are plotted in a vertical line on the extreme left of the chart and all the pure white ones in a line on the extreme right. All the shades are plotted in between, getting brighter from left to right and vice versa. The shape should never be a concern as it simply a reflection of the tonal ranges of the subject and setting you have been photographing – after all, a blackbird in snow will have a very different-looking histogram from a Snow Bunting on a black rock!

▼ Figs 2.5a, 2.5b and 2.5c
These histograms respectively show a well exposed image (a) with no clipping on either edge but at the same time tucked tight to the right-hand side; (b) is underexposed, being all bunched to the left; and (c) is significantly overexposed with a large spike/line up the edge of the graph.

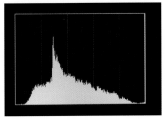 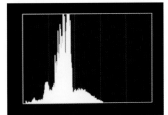 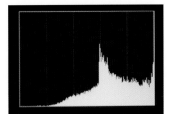

factual information you have – and not one reliant on the size or quality of the screen on the back of your camera – and is able to be quickly interpreted and adjusted as required, it is making best use of the digital information at hand.

▶ Fig. 2.6
Although there is a need to freeze the movement in the lower mandible of this singing Snow Bunting *Plectrophenax nivalis,* the image was still shot in aperture priority mode at a wide-open setting of ƒ5.6. At ISO 400 this gave a shutter speed of 1/640sec, which was the fastest possible and has done the job required. If a faster shutter speed had been needed, simply increasing the ISO to 800 or higher would have achieved this.

FOCUSING MODES

Although the terminology used by different manufacturers may vary, there are in essence two different focusing modes that you need to understand.

One shot (or single shot)

In this mode, when you partially depress the shutter the camera focuses on whichever focal point you have selected and, while your finger remains on the shutter before you complete the process by pressing it fully to take the picture, remains at that precise focusing distance. If you or your subject move during this time it will be out of focus. This mode is generally ideal for static subjects.

AI Servo (or continuous)

In this mode you focus initially in the same manner but, providing your finger remains partially pressing the shutter release button, it will continue focusing on the chosen focal point. If the subject moves it will track it and maintain focus. This mode is generally ideal for moving subjects – pretty much all aspects of bird photography fall into this category so it is the recommended starting point, but only once you are comfortable with the selection of your focal point in the first place.

FOCAL POINT SELECTION

Learning how to select the individual focal points on your camera will be one of the biggest step changes that you can make in achieving sharp and well-composed images.

When you look through your camera you will see a selection of individual focal points (usually in the form of small squares) formed in a generally oval shape in the middle of your viewing screen. Depending on your model of camera, this can range from around nine or so points to over fifty, but all generally clustered in this central area. Left to its own devices (leaving all the individual focal points active) your camera will generally look for the area of greatest contrast that it can find within the area of focusing points and focus on that, making it the critically sharp element of your image. The problem with this is that it will be drawn (in this subject instance) to either the edge of a bird and the contrast with a background or even a branch, rather than the head or ideally the eye, which is where the critical focus should almost always be. In order to achieve this you need to switch the focusing mode of your camera so that you can select individual focusing points. You can then pick the one that combines the best composition while at the same time focusing on the eye or head of the bird (depending on its proximity and therefore size).

Some cameras will have a multitude of other focusing modes in between these extreme settings, and some of them (especially one that allows you to include focal points surrounding the one selected) are especially useful when it comes to flight photography (*see* Chapter 6). Learn the range that your camera offers; flexibility and speed are key to good creative bird photography when it comes to moving the focal point around.

▲ Fig. 2.7
The individual focal point selected for this sleeping cygnet was placed over its eye, ensuring that when it eventually opened it from its slumbers this key part of the image would be sharp and, given the narrow depth of field, the feathers of its surrounding siblings' bodies would be out of focus.

VIDEO

Although it isn't photography in the classic sense, it is worth touching on the area of video as the vast majority of digital SLRs now offer HD quality video capabilities at the press of a button. Although the resolution of this footage does not match that of a full-sized RAW file, it is increasing significantly. At an impressive fifty frames per second in terms of capture rate, there will be many more individual frames to select an action shot from than on the fastest burst rate of still images. At the moment the individual frames you can pull out of video footage like this are really only of web usage quality, but who knows where this will end.

Learning how to quickly switch into video mode on your SLR will give you the chance to capture some moments in a very different way, and if you are producing talks, slideshows or have your own website they offer a welcome addition to the mix. Auto focusing does not work with most SLRs operating in video mode; it tends to work at its best where you have activity that you can film from a static base (i.e. a bird feeding or preening) or within a flat plane of focus (i.e. a bird swimming left to right).

Video is an area that camera manufacturers are concentrating on in their efforts to make SLRs increasingly versatile. Understanding its capabilities will ensure you stay up to date with new possibilities as they unfold.

Chapter 3

The Importance of Light

The Greek derivation of the word 'photography' literally means 'painting with light', which provides a pretty big clue as to the importance of understanding light and how it works when it comes to creating images. For many forms of photography lighting is under the control of the photographer, but in the natural world and especially when it comes to bird photography you have to work with what you are given or have the patience to wait for. There is no doubt that great light can transform an image, but other lighting conditions create different opportunities as well, so having an understanding of the different types of light and what sort of images can work in that light will help reduce the downtime days and remove any excuse to stay at home.

▼ Fig. 3.2
Taken at the Ladd S. Gordon Wildfowl Refuge in New Mexico, this image of a large flock of Snow Geese *Chen caerulescens* heading off from the cornfields where they feed during the day gains much of its impact by virtue of the stunning light created by a late, low afternoon sun providing warmth to the image, which is further emphasized by the dark storm clouds in the background. Taken on a duller cloudy day the image would have been flat and consequently less inspiring.

◀ Fig. 3.1
Red Grouse *Lagopus lagopus* calling from late summer heather in the early morning sunshine in the Derbyshire Peak District.
Canon 1D Mk4, 500mm + 1.4x converter, ƒ5.6, 1/1000sec, ISO 400.

▲ **Fig. 3.3**
The early morning light falling on this male Pine Grosbeak *Pinicola enucleator* photographed in northern Finland was coming almost directly over my shoulder as I took the image. The result is a completely even light across bird and perch, and that lovely catch-light in the bird's eye helps bring it to life even more.

DIFFERENT TYPES OF LIGHTING

Front Lighting

When I bought my very first camera as a teenager, back in the days of film and slide, the advice I was given in the shop was to make sure that I always had the sun at my back. If you want the most even possible light on your subject, bringing out feather detail and colour, this advice about front lighting stands the basic test of time. As front lighting is even in nature, it will be easy to ensure an accurate exposure. What good front lighting does require, though, is for the sun to be low in the sky, so that it

is shining directly onto the scene rather than from almost directly overhead, as is the case in the middle of the day (and especially so in the summer months).

Side Lighting

When positioning yourself to photograph a bird or a particular background, it is not always possible to stand with the light coming directly from behind you, and it may come in from the side. Side lighting like this is very popular with landscape photographers as it creates a real sense of depth, detail and contrast between the shadows and illuminated areas of the image. This can still work very effectively when it comes to bird photography, as carefully controlled contrast can emphasize the texture of any

▲ Fig. 3.4
This pair of Ravens *Corvus corax*, unusually allowing comparison of the subtle plumage differences of both the male and female of the species, was photographed in late afternoon with light coming into the image from the right-hand side. The low nature of the light ensures that all the feather detail in the lit parts of the bird (revealing much more tonal range than the simple description of black that might normally be applied to them) is really clear. The unlit side of the birds disappears into relative shadow.

lit plumage by drawing even greater attention to it. The challenges of getting the right exposure in these conditions of high contrast between the lit areas of a subject and the shadow areas can be significant. In these circumstances it is critical that you are constantly checking your histogram to ensure you avoid overexposing the key elements of the image, which will be those areas of your subject in the light.

Backlighting

There are occasions when having the light on your subject coming directly at you and therefore lighting the subject from behind offers a wonderfully creative and atmospheric alternative to the more conventional lighting approaches described above. If the key elements in this approach are correctly applied, the results can be very evocative: the sun must be low in the sky, a dark background is necessary to emphasize the halo or rim-lit effect around your

▶ Fig. 3.5
These two Puffins *Fratercula arctica* photographed in the late evening light on Skomer Island, Pembrokeshire, are photographed using back lighting from the setting sun, which is shining from the back left area out of shot. The result is a halo of light around their heads and their bills becoming almost translucent as the sun shines through them.

subject, and you need to control your exposure carefully to ensure you keep some details in the shadows of your subject but without overexposing the halo of light around it too much. The creative use of backlighting is covered in more detail in a separate section in Chapter 7.

WORKING IN OVERCAST CONDITIONS

▲ Fig. 3.6
On a dull day, where the tonal range of the subject and setting is relatively narrow, the prominent white patch on this Capercaillie *Tetrao urogallus* will cause far less of an exposure blip than it would if the sun were out, making contrast much greater.

Extolling the virtues and impact of good light when it comes to taking good images does not mean that all is lost when it is an overcast day, particularly if it is bright and overcast. Overcast conditions may mean a flatter quality as far as the light is concerned and less contrast, but for some subjects and especially at certain times of the day this can be very benefi-cial. Reduced contrast makes the fear of over- or underexposure much less significant and on birds with small patches of white on otherwise very dark plumage (such as Great Tit or Capercaillie) the risks

associated with 'blowing' the detail in these brighter elements are significantly reduced.

The same applies when working with black and white seabirds such as Guillemot and Razorbill. You are likely to be photographing these species in the summer months (the only season they are ashore) and, with the midday sun at this time of the year at its absolute worst in terms of contrast, bright

▲▲ **Figs 3.7a and 3.7b**
The difference in lighting conditions in these two images is clear to see. In one the sun is full out, and in controlling the exposure on the bright white chest area of this Razorbill *Alca torda* much of the rest of the bird has ended up very black in nature; as a result no feather detail or even the bird's eye are visible. In the other, albeit a closer portrait but taken in overcast conditions, the exposure latitude is much less, so there is no difficulty keeping the whites white as well as capturing detail in the dark elements of the bird's plumage.

overcast days are definitely the best time during which to visit their colonies – assuming you can't be there for the absolute best light, that is, which comes at the beginning and end of the day.

It's worth remembering that overcast conditions do eventually come to an end and that the changeable light of those classic sunshine and rain days that so often follows is among the most dramatic to work with. A downside of duller days is that it will generally mean that you are unable to get particularly fast shutter speeds as a result of the low light levels. However, the continuing improvement of SLR performance when using high ISO values is making this far less of an issue.

THE GOLDEN HOURS

Photographers often talk about the golden hours – particularly landscape photographers for whom the quality of light and especially the nature of colour in any sky included in their images are especially critical. The same applies to bird photography. The quality of light in the first and last hours of the day is at its warmest and most flattering on any species and in any location. At a subconscious level we tend to respond positively to warm-looking images (maybe they make us feel warm inside) and the extra yellows and reds in the light at this time of day really play to this.

From a bird photographer's perspective the additional benefit that comes with working at this time

▶ Fig. 3.8
The Solway Firth, which straddles the western border between England and Scotland, offers a safe overnight roosting ground for overwintering Barnacle Geese *Branta leucopsis*. As dawn approaches they leave the estuary to head to the fields just inland from the shore to graze during daylight hours. Photographed from the northern shores, the subtle colours of sunrise provided an additional bonus to the need to be there early to capture the moment in the first place.

▲ Fig. 3.9
The beginning of the breeding season sees early morning shows of strength and showy displays from male Black Grouse *Tetrao tetrix*. These displays almost only occur in the build-up to and immediately after sunrise, which offers the additional benefit of some of the nicest light of the day.

▲ Fig. 3.10
This Grey Phalarope *Phalaropus fulicarius* was photographed at
around midnight in the archipelago of Svalbard. The quality of light
through the night in summer when the sun never sets is clear to see.

of day is that it is generally the time when species
are at their most active – skeins of geese leaving the
overnight sanctuary of the estuary to return ashore
for a day's feeding, busy woodland birds finishing
the day in search of food before a cold winter's night
ahead, or black grouse gathering at their lek pre-
dawn for an early morning display of strength in an
attempt to attract a mate.

Being out early or late and thus increasing our
chances of seeing species is reason alone to work
at the ends of the day; the light quality is often

just a welcome bonus. Seasonal and geographical
variations in how the sun moves in relationship to
the earth do mean that the nature and length of the
golden hour varies. In the UK the sun has less distance to climb in the sky during the winter months
and so it can often seem as if the golden hour lasts
for a far greater proportion of the day. Head further
north to the likes of Iceland and even further into
the Arctic Circle and in the summer months the sun
barely sets, if at all – the result as it slowly skims the
horizon is a golden hour that can last all night.

▶ Fig. 3.11
This pair of Kittwake *Rissa tridactyla* perched on a snow-covered cliff in northern Norway, after returning early to their breeding grounds to grab the best spot, were caught in the early morning light as the curve in the cliff slightly darkened the snow behind them. The result is a far greater contrast between the birds and their background and a more impactful image.

LIGHT ON THE BACKGROUND OR LIGHT ON THE SUBJECT?

As you learn to spot the almost constantly changing and varying nature of light, it becomes apparent that different combinations of front, side and back lighting can offer new opportunities when it comes to improving the impact of your images. There is another facet that needs consideration and explanation, and that is whether the light is falling exclusively on the subject and not the background, or vice versa. In the case of the former the chances are that this will result in an excellent image opportunity – light on a subject from whatever direction that illuminates all of its detail but at the same time avoids highlighting the background will ensure a good level of contrast and impact.

In these circumstances it is important to make sure that your exposure is spot-on as far as your subject is concerned (carefully checking the histogram as you work) and accepting that your background will be on the dark side – this is what provides the contrast in the image. There may even be occasions where you want to deliberately

▲ Fig. 3.12
In a similar way to the image in Fig. 3.11, this Puffin *Fratercula arctica* is captured in a pool of late evening light on an Icelandic cliff top. By underexposing the image by around two full stops, which helped keep the whites under control too, the background of the distant cliff behind the bird has been rendered completely black. The result is a warm and impactful contrast between bird and setting.

 Figs 3.13a and 3.13b

These two images of a Siberian Tit, photographed in northern Finland, are taken on the same perch on the same afternoon – they may even be the same bird! In the first the light is shining on the bird from over my left shoulder looking into the image: it is not shining on the background. In the second the sun has moved lower and further round to the left and no longer shines on the bird and perch but rather on the background itself, changing its colour completely (it is the edge of a woodland) and resulting in a very different feel to the image as well as a much reduced shutter speed.

underexpose the image a little bit to make sure that the already dark background goes truly black, thereby increasing the intensity of said contrast.

Controlling the exposure when the situation is reversed (light on the background but not on the subject) requires you to ensure that the background is as bright as it can be without overexposing; this way you will retain the maximum amount of exposure and detail in the subject itself. This is generally a less pleasing style of image and harder to work with, but providing there is some colour in the pale background it can still be quite effective.

ARTIFICIAL LIGHT

There are very differing schools of opinion and approach when it comes to the use of artificial light in bird photography. There are, of course, times when it is completely essential, such as photographing owls at night; even the highest of ISOs are not going to allow you to work in the dark. It is also quite appropriate for the resulting images to look artificially lit, as it is clear that they will not have been possible to achieve without using flash.

The same applies to the careful and highly technical use of high-speed flash to freeze movement. Here, rather than relying on the shutter speed to do this, it is caught by illuminating the movement with a very short burst of flashlight, the result being that any motion pre and post the burst recedes into relative darkness and is therefore not recorded on your camera's sensor.

A typical hotshoe flashgun has a light burst duration of somewhere around 1/750sec to 1/1,000sec, but by reducing the power output of the flash this duration decreases in tandem, meaning that at 1/32 power it can be as fast as 1/10,000sec. The downside of this is, of course, that there is less light being output by the flashgun, but by moving it close to the subject and using a multiple flashgun set-up (often as many as five or six operating in unison may be required to illuminate, say, a hummingbird in flight, the flower it is hovering by and its background) it is possible to achieve the required light levels in tandem with the super-fast exposure times.

This is a highly technical aspect of bird photography worthy of a book in its own right, but a more everyday use of flashguns is using them on what is referred to as a fill-flash basis. Put simply, a small burst of flash is added to the exposure to fill in the details in the shadow areas of the subject. Ironically one of the best times to utilize this technique is during the middle part of a summer when the sun is almost directly overhead and a little additional controlled light can even out the huge contrast this creates. The amount of fill-flash you need will be determined by the depth of the shadows themselves (strong contrast needing more help from the flashgun) and the distance you are from your subject. SLRs work out exposure on a TTL (Through The Lens) basis with a compensation flash button working to override this – usually on the camera but on some models you may need to do this on the flashgun itself. A setting of –1 in terms of flash exposure compensation is generally a good starting point, then check the histogram as usual to adjust as needed. You should also move your flashgun away from its position directly above the camera in the hotshoe by using a cable, in order to remove the risk of red-eye caused by light reflecting from the bird's retina in its eye. There are various brackets that can be bought to do this when using long lenses.

Specialist extenders are available to add to your flashgun to magnify its output and thereby extend its reach – very useful given the distances you are likely to be working with in bird photography. Be careful, however: they are effectively magnifying glasses, so if left on for long periods of time can literally burn a hole in the front of your flashgun!

The use of artificial light does come with a warning. Its creative use, especially at the high-speed end, is unquestionable. But when it comes to using fill-flash, it is all too easy to get into a habit of using it on an almost constant basis. Not only is this not always good fieldcraft (some subjects may be more spooked by a burst of light at the same time as the noise of a shutter, rather than by the latter alone), but it can result in a certain sameness to your images. There is a great deal to be said at times for accepting the light conditions as they are and thinking creatively about how best to work with them. It can lead to a more varied portfolio over time.

▶ Fig. 3.14
Although this image was taken under controlled conditions and using a captive-bred Tawny Owl, the use of flash as the sole light source and the natural black background of a dark winter's night make this look a perfectly natural setting and shot – it's a bird of the night after all.

Chapter 4

Clues to Composition

This chapter is deliberately titled. When it comes to advice in the area of composition, it is not unusual to come across pointers being referred to as rules. There are no rules here, just clues and things to think about. Some of the most creative and inspiring images simply throw convention out of the window and approach composition in a completely different way, making them instantly more impactful. But if there is one overriding bit of advice when it comes to considering composition, it is to do it at the point when you are actually taking the image, rather than with the judicious use of the crop tool when processing it on the computer.

LANDSCAPE OR PORTRAIT?

Just because your camera happens to sit comfortably and logically in your hands in a landscape orientation (long side of the image running left to right) does not mean that this is necessarily the best way round to take your images. Even putting to one side the need to consider end-usage of your images (something which will certainly influence your decision on this matter) there are a multitude of occasions when rotating the camera round ninety

▲ Figs 4.2a and 4.2b
These two images of a Guillemot *Uria aalge* are identical in pixel count and taken from the same location and at the same setting on the cliff top. By rotating to a portrait orientation in the second image, however, the relative size of the bird in the image appears much bigger as it is positioned along the long side of the image.

◀ Fig. 4.1
Female Lesser Spotted Woodpecker *Dendrocopos minor* returning to her nesthole with a beakful of ant larvae, photographed in Bulgaria. Canon 1D Mk4, *f*6.3, 1/200sec, ISO 200.

▶ Fig. 4.3
This image of a Puffin taken on Skomer Island in Pembrokeshire appeared on the front cover of the RSPB's *Birds* magazine a few years ago. With a membership of 1.2 million members it is still probably one of my most widely seen images ever! Even though the Puffin's eyes are on the side of its head they are still prominent enough to ensure that there remains a sense of eye contact and of course the sand-eels, colourful beak and flower-laden setting do the rest.

degrees for a portrait orientation opens up a whole range of different compositional opportunities. If you have a camera with a second shutter release button to make this easier (*see* Chapter 1, 'Battery Grip') and are using a long lens on a tripod with a rotating collar designed to make this rotation less difficult as well, then ease of use isn't an excuse either.

SIDE ON VERSUS HEAD ON

When it comes to producing natural history shots of birds, and in particular where clarity of markings is essential to confirm or even on occasion help when it comes to identification of species (or even individual birds), then the classic side-on image of your subject is a necessity. From this perspective it is likely that any distinctive features on the head, wings and chest areas will be well recorded and the beauty of the bird captured to the full.

However, there are times, although it goes against convention, when images taken head-on to the subject can add a bit more character and personality to the shot. This is more typically the approach when it comes to mammal photography as many mammals have their eyes on the front of their faces and so a more intimate and engaging image can be achieved, especially if taken at eye-level. Birds, however, tend to have their eyes on the side of their heads and the eyes are often small and dowdy by comparison to other features, so they are not so automatically attractive from a head-on perspective. But, as has already been said, it is always worth breaking with these so-called conventions, because some birds in some settings and on some occasions just work when photographed head-on. It's hard to define just what makes this the case, but it seems to be where there is either a cheekiness of character or a familiarity about them, the need for identification perhaps becomes secondary to the personality on display.

▼ Figs 4.4a and 4.4b

These two images of the very familiar Robin *Erithacus rubecula*, both photographed on the same typically chilly winter's day, are, perch aside, quite similar in terms of balance, exposure, look and feel. The bird is the same one, too! The main difference is that in one the bird is side-on and the other head-on. Both have been used as magazine cover shots so clearly both have their commercial appeal, but I just feel the head-on one provides a little more insight into the character of the bird in question.

▲ Fig. 4.5
The background behind this Kingfisher, sitting patiently on the head of a reedmace, is created by the far bank of the river, a distance of some 20 or so metres away. Using a wide-open aperture and a 500mm lens along with a 1.4x converter, the bank is turned into a uniform brown background against which the subject really stands out.

THINK BACKGROUND

One of the most common mistakes made (and therefore easiest ways to improve) during the early stages of your development as a bird photographer is not giving due consideration to the background on which your subject is photographed. It is all too easy to become so absorbed and focused on the bird itself (it is after all what you want to photograph) that you fail to look at whether there is an out-of-focus branch behind it cutting right through its body, or if the even more distant shades of trees and hills behind create a colour change right through its head.

Poorly considered backgrounds are easy to miss when taking the picture but massively annoying when reviewing them; careful thought will ensure that they complement rather than distract from the main element of your image.

First of all, it's important to give due consideration to the lens that you are using. As discussed in Chapter 1, telephoto lenses compress perspective while wide-angle lenses exaggerate it, and the apparent depth of field in your image moves in tandem with this. What this means in practical terms is that even if you set up at a wide aperture such as f4 on a 50mm lens and are very close to your subject, a distant background will still have some defined

▲ Fig. 4.6
This Great Reed Warbler *Acrocephalus arundinaceus* photographed
in Bulgaria is a classic example of just how fine the line between a
perfect and slightly distracting background can be. The bird had a
favourite reed head he liked to sit and sing from and even stretching
my tripod to its highest point I couldn't avoid the line caused by a
change in foliage in the background. Left or right and I couldn't see
the bird, so this became an image of accepted compromise.

shape and form to it. On a 500mm lens at the same
aperture and taken from further away to achieve
the same 'in image' size of the subject, the same
background will disappear into an out-of-focus
colourwash.

Given that most bird photography is taken with
long lenses, this is likely to be the style of image you
will be taking and therefore it pays to appreciate
what makes a good clean background under these
circumstances. Firstly, when setting up a feeder,

stalking or approaching a subject or even working from a pre-placed hide, be sure to look behind
where your subject is and consider the background
in terms of clarity and colour. The further away it is
the better (this will render it even more out of focus)
and sometimes just a subtle change of position or
angle can avoid the incursion of unhelpful changes
of colour or horizon spoiling things. Changing your
height or moving marginally left or right can also
make a huge difference.

▶ Figs 4.7a and 4.7b
When this Black Guillemot
Cepphus grylle returned
ashore and settled on
this rock, as well as the
orientation decision (head-
on or side-on) I also had a
choice of backgrounds based
on where I chose to position
myself – the dark grey of
another boulder which
offered less contrast but a
more moody image or the
green of a grassy bank which
completely changed the feel
of the image. Backgrounds
really do make a difference.

There may be occasions when you have a background that is clean and complementary but by changing position a completely different colour of background becomes achievable, thereby changing the mood and feel of the image. Be aware of these possibilities and be prepared to change your position if you need to. Unless you are hide-based (and many of them are portable between one session and the next in some circumstances), avoid becoming rooted to just the one position. Look, too, for colours in the background that complement and contrast the colours of your subject.

The role of the background also has a key role when it comes to photographing birds on water – here it not only provides the colour for the background but also for the water itself. Selecting a corner of the lake where the water is still and where the light shining on any surrounding foliage is

◀ Fig. 4.8
This Coot *Fulica atra*, photographed on a local lake surrounded by a mixture of trees and houses, is set on a sea of gold caused entirely by the reflection of the surrounding foliage reflecting in the water. By placing the bird in the upper part of the image a uniform background has been achieved.

◀ Fig. 4.9
This winter plumage Long-tailed Duck *Clangula hyemalis* was photographed in a busy harbour in northern Norway where they often spend the winter months. Here a highly unusual and colourful background has been created by the reflection of a red and white building adjacent to the harbour, which I waited for the bird to swim into.

reflected in the water will give a uniformity of colour to your background if you need to have both water and foliage in it. It also gives you the opportunity to try out different compositions that make best use of the colour and at the same time avoid any messiness in the join between water and trees. Placing the bird in the upper part of the image avoids the need for a horizon and effectively turns the colourful water into a uniform background.

Although a clean background is generally desirable, there can be occasions where introducing some texture might give an increased sense of location or add another element to the image. A good example of this comes when working with shore birds on a beach. Uniform backgrounds are generally reasonably easy to achieve here, especially if you shoot from low enough to the ground, but when the bird is close to the water's edge and especially if there are

▲ **Fig. 4.10**
This winter plumage Sandwich Tern *Sterna sandvicensis*, photographed on the Atlantic coast of Florida, was enjoying a bathe at the water's edge at the end of another hot day. While focusing on the bird I was looking past him at the waves coming in from the right and pressed the shutter as they rolled into place to add some texture and depth and a real sense of place to the background.

some gentle waves behind it, using the shape of the waves and ensuring they are recognizable as such by a slight reduction in the aperture (say to ƒ8 or ƒ11) will add another element to the image.

The key with all of this is to make sure you are thinking about backgrounds as much as the subject and considering how best to use them to highlight the bird and its location.

RULE OF THIRDS

Back in the days when photography was dominated by film, people working on the processing machines in the high-street chemist, where much of the developing and printing was done, would have doubtless tired of the number of images that they saw of a small man in the middle of an image, in the middle of an empty landscape. The same would almost certainly have applied to most of the images they processed of people's first forays into bird photography – a small bird in the middle of the image with lots of empty space around it.

The rule of thirds, quite possibly something you will remember if you studied art at school, is a very simple and surprisingly helpful thought process to apply when it comes to avoiding this mistake,

◀ **Figs 4.11a and 4.11b**
In the second of these two images of a Crested Tit *Parus cristatus* you will see the so-called rule of thirds grid and how it has been used to help compose the image: the bird, in particular its key focal point of the eye, are placed at an intersection of the thirds and the overall balance of bird and perch is confined to the right-hand two-thirds of the image, leaving some balanced space on the left.

and helps to create a dynamic and well-balanced composition – something that is essential to help lift your image above being simply a record shot. The approach is very simple: it's a question of imagining a grid of two horizontal and two vertical lines each placed a third of the way across or up the viewfinder.

Some cameras will even allow you to add a viewing grid either on your screen or through your viewfinder that replicates this. The key then is to place the main elements of your image somewhere around

one of the intersections of the grid – the so-called hot spots of composition. If the subject is small in the frame this will be the whole bird, if it is larger it must be the eye. It is essential that the eye is sharp in bird photography as it is where the viewer of the image will first be drawn, often subconsciously.

Although you should never become a slave to this rule, it really is one of the most useful bits of compositional advice to work with and try to adopt subconsciously when setting up your image. A

▲ Fig. 4.12
At times a really tightly composed image can work really well, like this Dalmatian Pelican *Pelecanus crispus*, whose dynamic eye, bright orange pouch to his bill and wild-looking hair-do offer bags of character in this tight crop. Note that I waited until another bird drifted in behind to ensure a clean white background.

simple flick through any good collection of bird and other wildlife photographs with this template in mind and you will see it acting as a major influence.

One of the reasons beginners to bird photography find it hard to adopt the rule of thirds is that they are not comfortable (or quick enough) when it comes to moving around the individual focal points on their camera. As a result they find themselves reliant on the centre spot and think about cropping later. It is far, far better to learn to compose as you capture your images, moving the focal point towards one of the rule of third intersections based on where your key focal emphasis is required. Learning to see the picture in the field rather than at the computer will make you a photographer much more alive to different compositional opportunities.

▲ Fig. 4.13
I have deliberately cropped this image of a Black-Tailed Godwit *Limosa limosa* too tight, if only to make the point that without the space to breathe above and around it the bird feels really cramped inside the image.

◀ Fig. 4.14
Alone on a remote hilltop lek, this displaying male Black Grouse *Tetrao tetrix* has his sense of isolation significantly added to by his small representation in the image; positioning him in the corner and looking into the large amount of negative space only adds to this.

◀ Fig. 4.15
Bluethroat *Luscinia svecicus* are predominantly birds of the reedbeds, so capturing this displaying male on a stem and leaving plenty of negative space made up of the matching colour only goes to emphasize the sense of place and habitat.

USING NEGATIVE SPACE

With the first of the potential pitfalls of the little-bird-in-the-middle-of-an-empty-frame addressed by recomposing using the rule of thirds to introduce some dynamism, the thought process regarding said empty space changes dramatically. When the image is well composed, negative space becomes an extremely powerful compositional device, and is a natural extension in terms of your compositional thinking to the rule of thirds.

It is very tempting, particularly when you start using long lenses for the first time, to simply fill up the frame with your subject. After all, you've spent the money on the extra magnification and you want to get as big an image of your subject as you can, don't you? Sometimes the high impact of a frame-filling shot is undeniable, particularly when you get

the chance to really concentrate on the bird's face
and eyes; but most of the time you will be looking
to show all of the bird and if you end up with the
edge of the frame too tightly composed around it
the viewer is left with a feeling that everything is
cramped and constricted – the bird needs room and
space to breathe inside the image.

In much bird photography the habitat (whether
it be a simple perch, a heather moorland setting
or a colourful lake) is essential to telling the story
about your subject – placing it in context, as it
were. Negative space goes a long way to adding
this to an image, even when it's the colour-washed
background caused by a long lens, as the colour
alone will give a clear indication of the setting. There
are no hard and fast rules here – composition will
always have a degree of subjective judgement about
it – but don't be afraid to be really minimalist at
times. The old adage 'less is more' can often apply
when it comes to creating memorable and impactful
images.

WALKING/LOOKING INTO THE FRAME

Building on your subject's need for space and an
understanding of the rule of thirds, the next logical addition to the subconscious decision-making
process that this section is trying to develop is one
that involves the direction in which the subject
is walking, swimming, flying or looking. The key
here is very simply to make sure that it is looking or
moving into the negative (or other) space in the image. In other words, place the bird on the left-hand
vertical line of thirds if it is moving or looking left to
right, or vice versa.

▼ Fig. 4.16
This image, photographed in Svalbard, is a typical example of
ensuring that the space in the shot is composed in such a way that
the Kittiwake *Rissa tridactyla* is looking into it. To achieve additional
dynamism I waited until the bird decided to give one of its many
vocal calls, this time being rewarded with a highly unusual tongue
formation.

◄ **Figs 4.17a and 4.17b**
These two images of
Kittiwake *Rissa tridactyla* in a
similar setting to the one in
Fig. 4.16 demonstrate how
the dynamics of looking into
the space can be played with
for additional and perhaps
subconscious variation. One
bird is looking into the frame
even though its body is not
and the other bird's body is
looking into the frame but
its head is turned to look the
wrong way. Look for different
poses when faced with a
group of individual birds
looking seemingly identical.

One of the keys to making this thought process second nature is to ensure that you are both
comfortable and speedy when it comes to moving
your focal point around. Even an entry-level SLR will
have nine of these and the quick manoeuvring of
them towards the left or right of centre and maybe
even up or down to the intersections of the rules of
thirds should be something that simply happens as
soon as you see a potential subject to photograph,
almost in tandem with moving your lens to point in
the direction it needs to be to take the shot.

As with all aspects of composition, though,
sometimes playing with the viewer a little and looking for something that conforms to this approach
but at the same time doesn't can make even sitting
or resting birds much more dynamic in image
terms, such as the two Kittiwake in Figs 4.17a and
4.17b. Often you can find yourself sitting with quite

LOOKING LEFT TO RIGHT OR RIGHT TO LEFT?

With wild subjects and settings you do, of course, have no control over whether the subject is looking or moving from left to right or the other way round when it comes to taking your images. However, providing you have a clean background and the location is not recognizable in terms of its orientation, it becomes very easy to flip an image in post-processing so that the subject is heading in the opposite direction. Designers will do this all the time to suit a potential page layout, so should we worry or even consider this from a post-processing or even in-field compositional perspective? The English written word flows from left to right as we read it on the page and as a result this is the way our brains are wired to interpret things generally. It isn't therefore too much of a stretch to see that a bird moving that way will feel, however subconsciously, more natural than one moving right to left. The latter movement is more likely to induce a little more tension or discomfort for the viewer.

▲ Figs 4.18a and 4.18b
This is the same image of an American Oystercatcher *Haematopus palliatus* with one simply rotated round so the bird is looking the other way. Which one feels most balanced? It's a personal thing but I think (b) sits easier on the eye.

large numbers of birds to choose from in terms of subject material, all apparently sitting in the same sort of setting and doing the same sort of things.

Developing your eye to look around the group and spot those doing something slightly unconventional, such as these Kittiwakes, will give you the best chance of finding memorable and more interesting images.

ODD NUMBERS

Anyone who has ever spent any time having his or her images appraised by a Camera Club judge will be well aware of odd numbers as a thought process. Put simply, in much the same way as when you plant groups of similar plants in a flowerbed or pot, you should try to have odd numbers of birds in an image if you have decided to go for a number greater than two. Two works well if there is some obvious interaction between them (this can incidentally be negative interaction – i.e. looking deliberately away from each other, which tells its own story) but, above two, three, five and so on just has a more natural balance or feel to it. Much of this is at a subconscious level and again it might not always be practical or possible to group your subjects this way, but where you have the opportunity to do so it is a good method of setting yourself up.

▲ Fig. 4.19
To complete the collection of Kittiwake *Rissa tridactyla* in the same setting, here I deliberately composed to ensure that there were three birds in the image, creating a natural balance. As before, though, I have once again waited for that extra element that lifts the image, with the central bird giving another loud call, probably to the annoyance of its neighbours!

COMPOSING FOR IMAGE LIBRARY SALES

Although it is a market that has seen average returns per sale drop dramatically in recent years with the digital era changing the whole dynamic of supply and demand for bird images generally, for many people the idea of seeing their work in print and hopefully paying a little bit towards the cost of their hobby is likely to be best achieved by supplying your work to an image library. The whole area of preparing a portfolio for an image library is covered in more detail in Chapter 6, but when it comes to composing for general editorial use then using a simple checklist of possible image compositions can be a good way of ensuring that you get the most out of an obliging bird or opportunity.

Designers working with bird images always like to have plenty of space to work with, as they will very often be looking to add text in this space. They are also looking for images that work both as single page (and hopefully cover) shots as well as double-page shots. For the latter they will also need to take the join or page divide into account. The ideal combination of shots of any one bird sitting in a nice clean setting might then be:

Portrait – space above the bird
Portrait – space below the bird
Portrait – tight impactful shot (little space)
Landscape – space to the left of the bird
Landscape – space to the right of the bird
Landscape – tight impactful shot (little space)

Add in some of the twists to the compositional approaches already covered in this chapter and you'll see how with some thought to where and how you place your subject in the frame, and use the background generally, a whole array of similar yet varied images can be taken for an agency or one of its designer clients to choose from.

PARTLY SEEN SUBJECT

It isn't always necessary to see all of your subject in order to make an interesting image or one that tells a story about the bird in question. We have already established that the use of negative space around a bird helps to highlight the habitat it is in and can add significantly to an image, so spotting an opportunity to make even more of this habitat by having it mask part of the bird can add yet another twist or dynamic. Sometimes it may even be the only view you can get of a well hidden bird. Rather than let it put you off taking the shot, think about how the obscured view can actually help create the image. A classic example of this is a bird such as a Reed Warbler perched on a phragmites stem in the middle of a reedbed – as long as there is a clear view of the bird's head and eye, some defocused stems across it and around it can simply add to the sense of skulking secrecy that is typical of this particular species. Images that reveal only part of your subject also create an increased element of character or personality to the subject as well – whether it be the cheeky peek of a Red Grouse from its heather hiding place or a Purple Sandpiper dozing among boulders at high tide.

▶ Fig. 4.20
Purple Sandpiper *Calidris maritima* roost among rocks at high tide when their food sources made visible by the rising and falling tides are all covered. Not only can this make getting close to them quite difficult to achieve, but also they are likely to be partially hidden. Spotting the opportunity to place this dozing bird in the setting of the boulders, it was a question of focusing on his eye and waiting for him to open it briefly – something he would do quite regularly to ensure his general safety.

Chapter 5

Getting Started:
Some Project Ideas and Finding Locations

SET UP YOUR OWN GARDEN BIRDS FEEDING STATION

It might seem a very predictable place to begin, but trying to develop some bird photography opportunities literally on your doorstep has many advantages. Not only does it save time and the cost of getting to where your subject is, but it will also mean that you are able to be very responsive to what is happening in terms of the light and weather conditions as well as getting to know the subtleties of behaviour of your visiting species – all of these are key elements when it comes to creating images. The additional benefit of setting up a feeding station like this is that you will be able to create and manage the habitat and settings for the images as well, thereby increasing your involvement and at the same time acting as a great learning platform as to what works and what doesn't.

The starting point for creating a feeding station can be extremely simple – quite literally a pole feeder with your feed of choice (a high-energy seed mix is most likely to attract a reasonable array of species), and then underneath it attach a couple of natural perches either using a clamp or strong adhesive tape. I prefer to use the former, as it is flexible and less likely to get accidentally discarded. While birds are waiting for a space to feed directly on the feeder itself, they will become accustomed to resting and waiting on this perch for their turn to come around and this will provide the image opportunities.

▲ Fig. 5.2
While waiting for their turn at the feeder, birds will be content to sit on whatever branch you attach to it. Providing you compose your image to avoid including the feeder as well as the pole it sits on top of, you will have clean images and endless options of perches, too. Note how the perch is thin in nature (too thick and it dwarfs smaller garden birds), is positioned at an angle for compositional purposes and has been chosen in the first place because the leaves lie in the same plane of focus as the branch itself – important when working with the small depth of field these set-ups necessitate.

Where exactly to place the feeder in your garden is an important decision. Unless you have a particularly large plot, the chances are that you won't be able to go placing hides and the like to photograph from, so consider the door from your house to the garden or even the door of a shed as a place to work from.

Your final choice should be influenced by two key considerations – the direction that the sun moves during the course of the day and the nature of the background behind your feeder/perch combination. Bearing in mind that garden birds

◀ Fig. 5.1
Nuthatch *Sitta europaea* climbing on a silver birch stump at my feeding station at home in Shropshire. Canon 1D Mk4, ƒ4, 1/400sec, ISO 400.

▲ Fig. 5.3
The nice clean background behind this Blue Tit *Parus caeruleus* is provided by some trees at the bottom of the garden. The perch is attached to a feeding pole but deliberately angled upwards to provide some additional dynamic to the final image.

▲ Fig. 5.4
On a sunny winter's morning, overnight frost on a perch, in this case holly leaves, will melt quite quickly. I positioned this feeder and the attached perch so that the very first rays of the sun would fall on it during the shortest weeks of the year. All it needed then was a Blue Tit *Parus caeruleus* to arrive during the short window of opportunity when the elements were all in place.

are generally more active first thing in the morning (and coinciding with our desire to photograph in the best possible light), positioning the feeder so that front-lit, early morning light falls on it is probably the best starting point. This will also give you the chance to experiment with side lighting and maybe even backlighting throughout the day. Just remember that the angle the sun rises at does vary throughout the year; winter is generally the best season for feeder photography so base your choice on the position of the winter sun.

The final factor is to watch how birds behave in your garden before embarking on setting a feeder

up. Do they have a particular bush or tree where they like to sit or even congregate? Sighting your feeder near a safe zone such as this is important – most gardens have the occasional visit from a maraud-ing Sparrowhawk, so it is important for them to feel there is a safe place to bolt to. You'll also find that this will be where most of the birds approach and depart from your feeder, so if you are looking to catch some images of them landing on the perch (never easy, requiring a shutter speed of at least 1/1,000sec, pre-focusing on the landing spot and a huge amount of trial, error and patience) this will also be of importance in the setting up.

Regarding the background, you really need this to be as uniform as possible in terms of colour and it will need to be at least ten metres away to allow it to be rendered out of focus with the long lens that you are likely to be using. Not all gardens will allow this due to space constraints so, although it is a bit fiddly as they need setting up whenever you want to photograph, you can actually create your own background (*see* box).

The next element is the selection of your perch. Although the bird will be the main focal point of the final image, the perch on which it is resting is going to be the key difference between your image and the multitude of other images of Blue Tits, Greenfinches and Robins. When looking for a perch, try to imagine it once it's attached to your feeder. It will need to have some dynamism in terms of angles (avoid a dead straight stick), but at the same time needs to have a relatively flat profile so that it will sit comfortably within a narrow band of focus. Add in some colour and texture in the form of leaves, blossom, fruits, cones or lichens and you have something that should work well.

One other consideration that you might also bear in mind with regards to your perch is that many species are 'grab and go' merchants when it comes to visiting feeders. In order to encourage them to stay put in a favoured position on your perch, stick part of a seed-enriched fat cake to the back of the perch and they will sit still and feed in one spot for just a few extra seconds – time enough to get some images. In fact some species such as Long-Tailed Tits will only really be attracted to a garden feeder with the offer of some for these fat-based feeders, so having one either hanging off your pole feeder or nearby will be key to getting them to come to the garden in the first place. Take the fat balls away for the short time you are photographing and they will go straight to the fat on your perch.

Understanding what birds eat which types of food will attract the species you wish to photograph to your garden. In the same way that Long-Tailed

CREATING YOUR OWN BACKGROUND

If space is restricted in your garden, especially when it comes to getting a nice clean background, then attaching a scrim net, camouflaged sheet or even a blanket between two poles and hanging it behind the perch you wish to photograph the birds on is an alternative solution, even if not a very natural one. The key here is that it must be of a matt texture so that there is no reflected light bouncing off it or highlighted spots of light in the background of your images.

▲ Fig. 5.5
When I first put the permanent hide that this image was taken from in place, there was a flock of these Long-Tailed Tits *Aegithalos caudatus* in the nearby coppice so I was always hopeful that, with the careful use of fat-balls to attract them to the feeding station and strategically hidden pieces on the back of this lichen-covered branch, I would be able to get some images of one of my favourite garden visitors.

Tits love fat balls, Goldfinches are hugely drawn to nyger seed. A second feeder full of nyger seed is a simple way to target them as a species, should they be in the vicinity of your garden, but in the wild they are often to be found on teasels in the winter, prising seeds out with their delicate beaks. A teasel attached to a garden pole with nyger seed carefully placed

▲ Fig. 5.7
Although a little bit cheesy and perhaps unnatural in its setting, the careful placement of some seed and nuts in a small hole in the soil positioned between this group of snowdrops in a wide flat plant pot didn't take this Great Tit *Parus major* very long to find and allowed this image to be taken. Note how the hole (and therefore the positioning of the bird) and the snowdrops are such that they are all in a relatively similar plane of focus.

▲ Fig. 5.6
This is a classic image of Goldfinches. Careful placement of their favoured nyger seed in the rear of the teasel encouraged them to visit it to feed and even queue up underneath the seed head itself, waiting their turn, even though at times this could lead to some dramatic squabbles.

in the rear of the seed head (and out of sight of the camera) will attract them photographically in the same way as the fat on the perch does the Tits.

If you have enough space in your garden, or if you are trying to set up a feeding station in a nearby woodland or farmland location, then another option is to use a table as a staged feeding area. If you simply want something for, say, the winter, a wallpaper pasting table will be fine; for longer term use (wallpapering tables warp quite badly after a lot of rain) something more substantial will be required. The careful placement on the table of logs, tree stumps, piles of autumnal leaves or maybe even a

roll of turf to replicate a lawn will create a range of different environments for your garden birds to be set in. Carefully placed and regular feeding on the table will encourage the birds to visit it as well as the feeding poles you need to leave set up around it; removing the poles for the short time that you are photographing means they will know where to look for their nourishment.

If you want to attract the particularly photogenic and popular Great Spotted Woodpecker, use short lengths of tree stumps as natural feeding posts: a two-metre or so length of, say, a silver birch is perfect. It can either be put in place by digging a hole in the ground for it, or if you need it to be more portable then place it in a bucket of quick dry cement to hold it in place with a flat base. On one side of the trunk, and at a height based on where (and at what height) you will be taking images, drill a few small holes and then regularly fill these with a

ADD A SIMPLE REFLECTION POOL

Once you have an established feeding table you could consider introducing a simple pool area to allow you to achieve some reflection shots of the birds as they feed. The classic low-level infinity pools are large constructions containing a lot of water (and therefore requiring a lot of space and support), but a simple pool made from a sheet of mdf board, some wooden batons attached around the edges and a sheet of pond liner tacked carefully across the piece as a whole is ideal to start with. Having built the small pool, it can then be introduced to your table area in much the same way as any other new stump or log. Fill it with water as full as you can. If you want this to become a regular drinking pool for birds rather than just a photographic prop, you will need to change the water on a daily basis – once it gets too warm it will be used by birds in much the same way as a drinking or bathing ornament in your garden.

You want to attract birds to the rear of the pool, so this is the area where you need to introduce food regularly, adding moss, bark or leaves to ensure the pond liner itself is hidden from view, and carefully placing the food in amongst them for the birds to find. As with all new set-ups it's best to get things in place and let the birds work it out for themselves for a week or so before you look to start photographing.

▲ Figs 5.8a and 5.8b
Although depicted here on a workmate, this small reflection pool is an ideal starting point for taking images of birds at the water's edge. Before you decide on the size (in particular the length) of your pool, you need to ensure that it is long enough to give you a full reflection based on the angle and distance from the rear of the pool you will be photographing from: the greater the angle, the shorter the pool can be. The careful placement of moss (Fig. 5.8b) provides an area for the birds to land, feed or drink from and also gives the pool a natural-looking edge.

▶ Fig. 5.9
This stunning male Bullfinch *Pyrrhula pyrrhula,* photographed in South Yorkshire, was attracted to this man-made reflection pool by sunflower seeds hidden behind the bark used to hide the pool edge. Look carefully and you will see some seed husks on the water's edge from some he has already eaten.

mixture of peanuts and fat. Turn these holes to the back of the tree out of sight. Once again, it won't take long for any visiting woodpecker to make this their regular feeding spot, although restrict the food to just peanuts at photography time to avoid getting fat smeared on the bird's beak.

VISIT RSPB OR WWT RESERVES

We are very fortunate in the UK to have several large charities focused on wildlife and, in particular, birds. The Royal Society for the Protection of Birds (RSPB) alone has a membership in excess of 1.2 million people. Along with the Wildfowl and Wetlands Trust this level of support (and funding) means that they are able to be significant landowners and their locations and sites are very often well set up to accommodate visitors with an array of hides. Some of them such as the WWT's Barn Elms site are even in the middle of cities (in this case London), so are even accessible by public transport. And there are reserves such as Bempton in North Yorkshire where no hides are even necessary to see and photograph the seabirds that colonize the cliffs there.

Many of these reserves are set up and positioned with bird-watching rather than bird photography in mind and as a consequence can be facing into the sun, at a high and unflattering angle from a photographic perspective or simply too far away even with a telephoto lens to be able to take any worthwhile images – binoculars and telescopes have much greater reach than most lenses. Having said that, however, there are many hides on reserves that are well worth visiting, are well positioned or work well at certain times of the day or year based on light conditions or species density and, given that the cost of annual membership to these organizations gives you access literally every day if you wish, they represent another excellent way to expand your

▲ Fig. 5.10
Peanuts, fat and peanut butter in varying ratios embedded in some holes drilled into the back of this silver birch trunk were irresistible to this male Great Spotted Woodpecker *Dendrocopos major*. The holes were carefully drilled to be just out of shot and when I was photographing I avoided the fat and peanut butter so that there weren't smears or lumps that could stick to the beak.

portfolio as well as your photographic and observational skills.

When it comes to choosing a reserve to visit, deciding when to go and how to approach your day there if it is your first time, there are some simple steps that will make sure you will get the most out of it. First, do your research before you go. This comes

▲ Fig. 5.11
Close-up views of over-wintering Whooper Swan *Cygnus Cygnus*
are achievable at a number of WWT reserves including Martin Mere
and Caerlaverock. There are feeding times published on the reserve
websites; also look at the maps to see which way the sun will be at
the main hides where this feeding takes place, so you can decide if
the morning or afternoon one will offer the best light conditions.

in the form of reading as much as you can about the
location – they will all have pages on the internet – with a view to finding out what the reserve's
main focus is species-wise and therefore when
you should be looking to visit. The seabirds will not
be at Bempton breeding in the winter months, but
visit the WWT reserve at Caerlaverock at that time of
year and the over-wintering Whooper Swans and
Barnacle Geese will be.

A further aspect of research, especially if you're
trying to choose between a couple of different reserves, is to use the internet to search for images that

have been taken there. You can do this by using any
search engine, or even visiting some of the leading
wildlife image libraries and using their search tools
to enter the reserve's name. Although no entries
doesn't necessarily mean it isn't worth visiting, finding several almost certainly means it is.

It's also worth checking the site entry times too –
many are effectively open access so it is possible to
be there for sunrise and that lovely morning light; if
the website is unclear they are generally more than
happy to help if you phone them. Make sure you
have checked the sunrise and sunset times, too, as

▶ Fig. 5.12
This image of an Avocet *Recurvirostra avosetta* was photographed from one of the main bird-watching hides at the RSPB reserve at Titchwell in Norfolk. When I arrived at the reserve I met a couple of other photographers (whom I didn't incidentally know) and they tipped me off that this one was regularly feeding in front of the hide. It pays to ask and engage in conversation when working a reserve or popular spot.

well as any high or low tide times that may impact on the habitat and how the birds behave. There's no point visiting a coastal mudflat for feeding waders as the tide is falling as they will be heading away from you; look rather for a rising tide coming up to your viewpoint when the light might be at its best. If you can find a map of the site before you go it will be worth looking at the location of each and every hide, seeing what habitat is likely to be immediately in front of it and most importantly what the direction of the light will be as the day starts and progresses.

Finally, before you go check the local area's bird-watching sightings website (again this will be easy to find using a good online search engine) as it will give an indication of anything unusual that's been seen there recently. On arriving at the reserve the same thing should be done by checking the latest sightings board that will be somewhere near the entrance or reception desk, if the reserve has one. At the same time, asking a warden or volunteer what's about and which hides they recommend from a photographic point of view will hopefully confirm if not add to the information you have already gleaned.

It will then be a question of following your planned route and giving each setting a decent amount of time. If you see other photographers there, be prepared to ask what's about and where they might have had some success already that day. After the inevitable 'you should have been here yesterday' tales, there will always be some snippets of useful advice, as most fellow photographers are generally all too keen to help, especially if they know the reserve well.

The last element to working a reserve is make sure you go back. Then go back again. The point being that the more times you visit somewhere and the more time you spend there generally, the more you will come to understand how the reserve works, how the birds move around as the day progresses, the tide rises and falls, the seasons change and as a result where the best places to be are and when.

DON'T BE AFRAID TO VISIT THE SO-CALLED HOT SPOTS

Having highlighted the benefits of visiting established reserves, there is on occasion a certain snobbishness that can be found about the images that are captured there, the perception being that it isn't a reflection of your photographic or fieldcraft credentials as a bird photographer if that is where you are taking your pictures. Never let that be a reason not to visit any location.

So-called hot-spots are given that description for a reason – they offer good, and very often great opportunities for bird photography. While you are in the process of developing both your skills and your

◄ Fig. 5.13
This may only be a classic shot of a Red Kite *Milvus milvus* in flight taken at the best (and most popular) feeding and photographic site for them in the UK at Gigrin Farm, but when it is your first such image and if it has taken you a number of visits to get the blue sky background that you wanted, let alone the skills you needed to hone to capture a fast-moving bird in flight, then it is still a great image to have captured.

▶ Fig. 5.14
The spring high tides on the Wash during the autumn and winter in particular cause huge numbers of waders, principally Knot *Calidris canutus*, to gather in the large pools on the reserve. Each tide is different in terms of numbers and of how the birds behave, so, because the photographic conditions change constantly as well, it took many visits before I managed to capture this frame-filling image. There are many other such high tidal roosts around our coasts, but Snettisham is a so-called hot-spot as it is easily accessible, reasonably predictable and when it all works simply very good in terms of the experience and photographic opportunity.

portfolios (processes that never end, incidentally), these are excellent places that should be high on your must-visit list.

The logic of visiting a reserve on a regular basis applies equally to working your garden feeders throughout the year. The more you go, the more you see and understand how the place works. You recall which images you liked and which you didn't from your last visit, allowing you to experiment and try new things or work on improving certain types of shot. The weather conditions will change, presenting new challenges but also new opportunities, and you will carry on building your experience and knowledge of both the photographic side of things and your subjects. Once you know a hot-spot well you will not only be able to make the most of it, but you will also be that helpful photographer you met the first time you visited and asked for some advice.

FOCUS ON SEABIRDS IN THE SUMMER

One of the undoubted highlights of the UK when it comes to bird photography is our vibrant seabird colonies. Many serious bird photographers from continental Europe come to our coasts during the summer months to visit our cliffs and take full photographic advantage of what they have to offer. We are blessed with many of the continent's biggest

▼ Figs 5.15a and 5.15b
It is important to know exactly where any bird species that you want to photograph is likely to be in its annual life cycle at the time you choose to photograph it. This Guillemot *Uria aalge* filled ledge was photographed in early May **(a)** when the birds were guarding newly laid eggs, and then again in late June **(b)** when the chicks had hatched and were growing well but not quite ready to fledge. Visit a month or so later and the cliff would be deserted.

and most accessible colonies of Puffins, Guillemots and Razorbills (Skomer Island in Pembrokeshire, the Farne Islands off Northumberland and multiple locations in the Shetlands), along with Gannets and cliff-nesting gulls such as Kittiwakes or coastal nesting colonies of Arctic Tern all offering an almost endless array of image opportunities. Add in the sights, smells and sounds of a seabird colony and for bird lovers who enjoy their photography there really can't be many better places to be during the summer months.

All these species are only really ashore for about three months of the year, spending the winter either at sea or in the case of terns migrating to warmer climes, so it is really only from the end of April through until late July/early August that the opportunity to work with them is available. The list of locations is too long to detail here, but among the highlights on any list should be Skomer Island in Pembrokeshire (excellent for Puffin photography), Bass Rock in the Firth of Forth (a huge accessible Gannet colony, with the added bonus of flight and fishing photography on some of the trips there), the Farne Islands off the Northumberland coast (Arctic Terns, Guillemots, Razorbill and Puffins on Inner Farne as well as Staple Island, which is particularly good for Puffin flight photography), and a whole array of colonies in the Shetland Islands dependant on your species focus.

Although our summer weather is very variable and many of the best colonies are based on islands around our coast, meaning that the winds need to be in the photographer's favour to get to see them, with some careful planning both in terms of the logistics of getting there as well as the precise time you choose to go, based on the nature of behaviour and activity you want to focus on, this really is a subject area that you can get well stuck into and build over many summers.

The whole area of developing a portfolio in terms of depth and breadth is covered in more detail in Chapter 7, but British seabirds with their wide range

▲ Fig. 5.16
A search on the internet will reveal an array of boat companies offering day trips out to the Farne Islands. A number of these offer extended full day outings for photographers that give you maximum time ashore and also the best chance to be there in the less harsh light early and later in the day. It pays to do your research when planning such a trip.

of species represent an ideal opportunity to do both. Some of these will be relatively easy to photograph and some considerably harder – Black Guillemots are probably the hardest of the four breeding auks to find here in the UK (the RSPB reserve on Mousa in the Shetland Isles is probably the most reliable public site), and for species such as Great and Arctic Skua a trip to the Shetlands is also required. You can then capture them in a variety of settings, conditions, points within the life cycle of their short time ashore, as well as experiment with a wide variety of photographic styles.

Most seabirds, especially those in large colonies well used to big numbers of visitors on a daily basis, are surprisingly tolerant of human presence. The most accessible colonies will have a warning rope for you to stay behind but this will generally be just a few short metres from where the birds are breeding. As a result seabirds are an excellent area to focus on even if you haven't made the major step of investing in a 500mm or similar long telephoto lens; good images can easily be achieved with a mid-zoom and there will also be plenty of wide-angle opportunities. Add the chance to try flight photography into the mix and it really is a great subject area to try out many of the approaches outlined in this book.

◄▲ Figs 5.17a and 5.17b
A day spent in a colony of
Gannet *Sula bassana* can
result in an array of images
including wide-angle
context-setting shots
and birds in flight, in this
instance bringing in some
more nesting material.

▲ Fig. 5.18
Although this image was taken in the dramatic setting of the Cairngorms, the fact is that these were very tame Mallard *Anas platyrhynchos* who were happy to come very close to me in return for some bread and seed, making this an image replicable in a multitude of locations close to where you live.

LOOK FOR LOCAL OPPORTUNITIES

One of the easiest mistakes to make when it comes to bird photography is to believe that you have to travel great distances in order to find good subjects worth spending time photographing. Hopefully the section on setting up your own garden bird feeding station earlier in this chapter has given you an indication that there is always plenty to do on your own doorstep, even if you live in a town or don't have a garden to undertake such a venture.

There are birds to be found literally everywhere and with a little thought they all offer the potential for capturing images. Every town will have a pond, lake or canal that will attract an array of birds – Mallards (much underrated; if they were less common we'd rave about the intensity of some of the stunning colours in the male Mallard especially), Mute Swans, Coots and Moorhens all offer opportunities to practise your techniques and develop your skills and creativity (*see* Chapter 7).

There are other advantages to working with birds in well populated locations such as these – the chances are they will be very used to people being around them on a daily basis. As a result they will be a lot more approachable and give you more photographic opportunities. Looking around locally, you will soon develop a series of places that are good at certain times of the year or under certain weather conditions and all within a short distance of home, so that when some of the dramatic weather conditions that we occasionally get arrive you will know precisely where you want to head to and what you

▲ Fig. 5.19
This image of a Great Crested Grebe *Podiceps cristatus* parent feeding a youngster on the nest under the protection of its partner was taken without the need for a hide and from the side of a small lake in the middle of a well-developed housing estate in Telford, Shropshire. Although I had spent most mornings of the preceding six weeks visiting and photographing them, I wasn't alone as early morning dog walkers and joggers would regularly pass by, meaning that the birds were used to a level of activity or general disturbance in their habitat.

will be able to photograph there to make the most of them.

Having already encouraged you to look for bird reserves around the country, the same logic applies to all local reserves as well. Your local Wildlife Trust will have a website detailing where they are, as well as what can be found there and when. It's often worth a first visit, even without a camera, just to get a feel for the places that look interesting. Look for local bird-watching websites on the internet too, as they will have plenty of up-to-date information as to what has been spotted and most importantly where; locations cropping up regularly on the sightings page are worth exploring as well.

Finally, be prepared to find bird photography opportunities literally anywhere – even the local landfill and recycling centre can throw up the chance to photograph Gulls and show just how well they have adapted to taking advantages of our waste. Just make sure you've asked the site management for permission to photograph there.

▲ Fig. 5.20
This image was taken within just a few miles of my home. When the overnight snowfall greeted me that morning I knew just which ponds I wanted to visit to see how the local waterfowl such as this Coot *Fulica atra* might be faring.

ATTEND A BIRDS OF PREY PHOTOGRAPHY WORKSHOP

Although the idea of working with captive subjects might not necessarily fit comfortably with many purists, there are without doubt a large number of benefits to be had from attending and photographing at a well-run and organized workshop of this type. As long as you are clear in any subsequent usage of your images as to the circumstances around where and how the shot was taken then the first of these is that you will have an unprecedented amount of time and proximity to what would otherwise be particularly difficult birds to photograph.

Although working with Kestrels or Barn Owls may well be the sort of projects you wish to progress on to, these require a considerable amount of fieldcraft, time and application, some of which is covered in Chapter 8 of this book. In the learning stages of the art and techniques of bird photography, though, this is likely to be a step too far, so time spent with the species under controlled conditions offers the chance to not only see them up close (an experience in its own right) but the time to think about all the different compositional elements already covered, with a subject that you know isn't going to be taking to the wing a few seconds later. You will have time

▲ **Fig. 5.21**
The chances are that, if you were to find a Barn Owl *Tyto alba* using an entrance to an old stable building such as this, it would be nesting inside. Given that they are a protected species, a Schedule 1 licence would be required to work there photographically. This image however, captured on one of my own Bird of Prey workshops, gives the same image opportunity to all attendees and without any risk of disturbance to a wild bird either. It's also a fun shot to have in your portfolio!

to consider the rule of thirds, time to consider your backgrounds, time to experiment with different lenses, time to play with different depths of field and time to see how changing the angle of the light will impact on your images.

Well-run days will offer a number of different species and settings, all of which should be well considered and appropriate to where the bird might be found in order to help naturalize the overall image. Good workshop leaders will also ask you to let them know what you are looking for from them during the course of the day, and be able to offer practical and compositional advice.

ATTEND A ONE-TO-ONE OR BIRD WORKSHOP OR PRIVATE PHOTOGRAPHY HIDE

Such is the massive increase in popularity of bird and all other aspects of wildlife photography these days that a large number of private hides and professional or semi-professional photographers offer the opportunity to spend a day photographing with them or visiting one of their established hides and set-ups. Although at face value these can often look quite expensive, there are many obvious advantages.

To start with, much of the hard work and field-craft required to create the opportunity will have already been done for you and in today's time-poor society that has an obvious attraction. Nature still needs to play her part and perform on the day, whether it be the species in question or the light and weather generally, but your odds are massively increased in terms of achieving something quickly.

Good hides and set-ups will have already taken into account much of the preparatory work covered earlier in this book – for instance, backgrounds, perch selection, light direction – and some of the subtle feeding techniques designed to encourage birds to visit the most photogenic of settings will have been practised for many weeks or even months prior to your visit.

While some hide set-ups simply present the photographic opportunities for you to take advantage of, there are others, both hide-based and not, that involve spending time with the photographer who has organized the day for you. The potential benefits here are not only the photographic opportunities of whatever the day you've chosen promises, but also the chance to pick the brains of the expert in question. It is important, therefore, to go armed with a bit of a mental checklist of things to discuss or ask about during the course of the day, and be prepared to engage in as much questioning dialogue as you can. When you first meet up, a good coach in this field will tend to ask you what you are looking to achieve from the day in terms of learning as well as your final images.

Choose a photographer whose work you like and admire, particularly if his or her experience includes the subject you will be photographing or the location you will be working in. Look beyond the two or three images they use to promote the day at their online galleries or blogs to see that they have a depth of coverage and an overall standard that you might aspire to. You also need to decide if you want a one-to-one approach or might benefit from having another attendee like yourself as part of a small group workshop – a kindred spirit if you like, who you might also get some advice and ideas from during the day. A good coach can become a good mentor and conduit through which your photography and portfolio can improve greatly, but it does pay to be objective in your assessments.

▶ Fig. 5.22
This Little Owl *Athene noctua* was photographed at a private hide. The birds nested in a large oak tree near the hide and would visit the array of fence posts in front of the hide to feed on strategically placed mealworms two or three times a day. Plenty of patience was still required as there were long periods of inactivity between visits, but these were nothing compared to the days and weeks of work required to get this behaviour and opportunity to work from scratch.

Chapter 6

Developing Your Portfolio

DEPTH OR BREADTH – A QUESTION OF PERSONAL OBJECTIVES

Once you have developed the skills required for impactful and creative bird photography, as well as the appetite to put in the hours necessary to achieve the level you are aiming for, then the direction in which you might wish to take it is very much a personal choice.

For some it may simply be a question of having as much breadth to their portfolio as they can. In much the same way as some birdwatchers have certain species they wish to add to their lifetime lists, many bird photographers have the same desires. If these hobbies overlap, this is a logical route in which to go and in this case involvement in the many bird rarity update sites and services available these days (such as Rare Bird Alert) will clearly have a role to play in achieving that objective; it's certainly not unusual to see as many 500mm lenses as telescopes at many rare bird gatherings these days.

For others, however, developing a greater sense of depth to their work and maybe even a greater variety to the style of their images is equally as important as the thrill and excitement of new species per se. Your focus can then become one of personal improvement, experimentation and the highs and lows that come from trial and error along the way.

▲ Fig. 6.2
I have countless images of Blue Tits *Parus caeruleus* on my hard drives but never tire of photographing them in different settings and seasons and seeing them exhibit different behaviours. For me, this is one of the key ways to build a portfolio.

SECRETS OF GOOD FLIGHT PHOTOGRAPHY

Flight photography is probably one of *the* hardest of all photographic skills to do well and consistently. It relies on a good eye, generally requires fast shutter speeds, excellent tracking skills (both the photographer when it comes to panning and following the bird and the autofocus capabilities of the camera/lens combination when it comes to staying 'locked on'), a good understanding of exposure compensation and the usual blend of perseverance and luck. The smaller the species, the harder all of this becomes, so it is worth getting your eye in with easily accessible and larger subjects – Swans and Geese at a WWT reserve, for instance. They tend to

◀ Fig. 6.1
European Roller *Coracias garrulus* calling to attract a nearby mate, Hortobagy National Park, Hungary. Canon 1Dx, 500mm + 1.4x converter, *f*8, 1/320sec, ISO 800.

▲ Fig. 6.3
Small birds like this male Kestrel *Falco tinnunculus* have very fast
wing beats, which require equally fast shutter speeds to freeze them
and fast focusing to keep up with them. This bird had just taken off
from the ground after a failed hunting attempt and was banking to
change direction, offering a brief chance to get locked on and press
the shutter.

be easier to focus on initially, appear to fly slower as
their wing beats are more considered, and they are
also less erratic in terms of their flight paths, making the predictive element of the process easier to
manage.

It is important to make sure you adopt a good
stance for flight photography. Unless you have very
strong arm muscles, you are likely to be using a
tripod when using a long lens like a 500mm, so it
is important that this is at a height that allows you
complete freedom to follow the subject and follow/
pan with it as it comes closer and flies past; you
don't want to be bending over and finding yourself
in an awkward position. Given the speed at which

all of this happens, using a gimbal-style head on
your tripod will give you the best flexibility as it will
allow panning both up and down as well as side to
side, while keeping both hands on the camera and
lens combination. If you are in a position both in
terms of good light conditions and also proximity
to the birds in flight to work with a shorter lens like
a 300mm, then handholding is a recommended
option as it gives complete freedom of movement.

Anticipation is an essential, and unless it is
simply a one-off opportunity it pays to spend time
watching how the flight activity in your chosen
location actually develops. Wind direction will have
a key part to play as birds will always look to take-off

▲ **Fig. 6.4**
Because this Gannet *Sula bassana* was gliding close by the cliff top
where I was standing, and because they are quite large birds that
often hang in the breeze when near their breeding colony, it was
possible to handhold the camera with a 300mm lens for maximum
flexibility.

or land into the wind, so if you are working at,
say, a seabird colony or a site where, for instance,
Osprey may be fishing you need to have the wind
behind you. In the case of the seabirds it is then a
question of watching for any regular patterns in
their approaches or routes, selecting a bird to follow
in at some distance and then looking to keep the
individual focusing point on the bird as it gradually
becomes the size you wish in the frame. It is far
better to pick it up early and wait until you press the
shutter for your burst of images, as it always takes a
while to lock on and it's better to do this before the
critical point rather than trying at that moment and
missing the shot. In terms of camera settings, the

highest burst of speed and the continuous focus
setting equivalent are required.

Compositionally, use a focal point just off centre
so that you can allow some space in the image for
the bird to be flying into. Remember, however, that
on most cameras the autofocus speed and accuracy
is not so good on the peripheral focus points, so
don't go all the way to the edge. A small amount of
cropping can complete the balance of your final
image if necessary.

In terms of lighting it is best to avoid the middle
part of the day (except perhaps in the winter months
when the sun is lower generally), as you want to
avoid having deep shadows on the underside of the

▲ Fig. 6.5
It was only on the third and final day's photography in this Finnish
hide that the wind finally moved round, so that when the fishing
Osprey *Pandion haliaetus* took off with his catch it was actually
towards rather than away from the camera!

birds' wings. A fresh covering of snow or heavy frost
works wonders here in terms of reflecting light back
onto the underside of flying birds, and these would
be good conditions to work in. Plain blue skies can
look a little similar and repetitive after a while, so
don't be put off photographing in broken cloud,
especially when it has its own colour shades to add
to the image.

Finally, be prepared to stick at it. This is a difficult
photographic technique that will take time to master,
and the margin between OK and great images is
very fine. When light and wind conditions are right
it really does pay to put in a shift working on your
flight shots. There may well be a lot of editing to do
later, but the cost savings of digital shooting make
that an affordable option.

▲ Fig. 6.6
This White-tailed Eagle *Haliaeetus albicilla* is made to look even more dramatic because of the storm lighting on both it and the cloud formations behind; a few moments later it poured with rain.

WORK A SPECIES
FOR A LONG
PERIOD OF TIME

Throughout the text of this book there has been an emphasis on getting to know your subject and the need for perseverance. One of the best ways to do this is to work with a species over a prolonged period of time and this can be achieved in a number of different ways.

Try to find a good site for a species, possibly close to home, meaning you are then able to visit on a regular basis and get to know where the birds like to be at certain times of the day, follow their patterns of behaviour and the life cycle of their courtship, breeding and parenting. While the image opportunities of the latter are obvious (although they do come with some essential fieldcraft and even legal considerations covered in Chapter 8), in terms of portfolio-building the most useful element to come out of this is the greater insight into behaviour that you will gain. It is only by spending time with individual birds or species that you learn to recognize the subtle nuances of how they go about their lives. Where this really becomes of benefit is when it comes to anticipating what they are going to do. Once you have spotted a pattern of behaviour or a tell-tale movement that comes before something like a shake of the feathers or preparing to take-off, you can position yourself ready for what is likely to happen.

Many bird species are seasonal in terms of the time they spend in our part of the world, making the amount of time it's possible to spend with them instantly restricted. It can therefore take several years of concentrating on them during these brief periods of the year before something approaching a portfolio starts to develop. While a one-off session with a species can be very rewarding, there is always scope for improvement – the weather conditions will be different, meaning a different mood or feel to your images, an appraisal of a first session's images will reveal sole shots that haven't quite worked and offer scope to improve on, and there will be image opportunities that simply never developed the first time.

A final consideration here is the opportunity in terms of experience that researching, finding and working at a number of different sites with the same species have to offer. Locating good sites was covered in the previous chapter, but applying the principles to particular species can provide a real focus to this preparatory work. Each site will offer something different in terms of background, habitat, setting and behaviour, even before the vagaries of weather and light are introduced, and give you more opportunities to learn about your subject and improve your photographic coverage of it.

▶ Fig. 6.7
Immediately after a shower finishes there is always another image opportunity close behind, as birds will look to shake all the excess water off their feathers. Given a nice dark background and a slow shutter speed, this is exactly what happened when this Red-footed Falcon *Falco vespertinus*, photographed in Hungary, decided it was time to dry off.

BE PREPARED TO TRAVEL FOR DIFFICULT DOMESTIC SPECIES

Whether on the grounds of rarity or scarcity, there are some species that are extremely difficult to photograph in your home country, even though they may be regularly recorded. Added to this are the issues of access in terms of where they may be and

the need for licences in the case of the Schedule 1 species at breeding time, when they may be at their most predictable location-wise. However, it's probably fair to say that somewhere in the world is a location where it's significantly easier to photograph every species. When it's one that you are particularly keen to spend time with for whatever reason, being prepared to travel overseas to do so is well worthwhile and should be seriously considered. The current increase in specialist photographic holiday companies makes this even easier to organize, although the same considerations should apply as when choosing a one-to-one workshop or private hide, and probably more so.

A good example of the sort of species this applies to is the Capercaillie. In the UK this is a declining species (because of shrinking habitat) and it also has Schedule 1 status, meaning that approaching it during the entire duration of its breeding season is illegal. In Scandinavia, however, it is a common

▼ Fig. 6.8

This Capercaillie *Tetrao urogallus* is displaying at his traditional lekking site in late spring and building up a harem of females around him – they only spend a few days together like this each year. The chances of working at a site like this in the UK are virtually nil with Schedule 1 licences and critically small numbers of the birds in the country, so visiting Scandinavia where they are a much more numerous species (this image was taken in Norway) is the only viable way to experience and photograph this species and its behaviour.

◀ Fig. 6.9
When the heavens opened, this Great Spotted Woodpecker *Dendrocopos major* feeding on this tree decided to push himself flat and sit out the downpour. The resultant image of his raindrop-covered head and body and the rain against the background is as dramatic as any I got of him on that perch all that winter.

species and like the rest of the grouse family one that it is perfectly legal to hunt. Although still difficult to find, working with the right local knowledge it is perfectly possible to spend time photographing these birds during the spring weeks when they are likely to displaying at their traditional leks – something that is beyond the reach of all bar a few here in the UK.

Although this adds a cost to your photography, the trade-off is having harder-to-achieve images in your portfolio (very relevant when considering submitting them to specialist image libraries or selling them generally), alongside some experiences both photographically and in other ways that would simply not be possible without making this step.

GO OUT IN BAD WEATHER

There is nothing that adds more depth to a portfolio or drama to individual images than when the weather become a major critical element. Although the importance of light remains key to good images, add in some snowy surroundings (or even falling snow) or a heavy downpour and, providing you are well protected in terms of your kit (and to a lesser extent your personal dryness), these are conditions in which even so-called everyday species look at their best and most impactful.

There are, however, a couple of considerations to make the most of what bad weather has to offer. When rain alone is the provider of the challenges, the most important thing is to find a dark background against which to place your subject. This is necessary so that the rain actually appears in your images – it will only show up when there is a high degree of contrast between its lighter shade and the background. Although it does vary based on the intensity of the rain itself and the general light levels, a shutter speed of around 1/125sec will normally render the rain as distinct streaks or lines in the background. Add a bedraggled-looking bird into the foreground and a story-telling image emerges.

Falling snow, often more of a challenge when it comes to driving than anything else, should be treated in the same way background-wise, but it is also worth noting that your camera meter is very likely to underexpose any image which is predominantly white. Using the exposure methodology described in earlier chapters, you will need to make

▲ Fig. 6.10
This image of a Golden Eagle *Aquila chrysaetos* photographed in the
mountains of Norway in winter demonstrates just what the right sort
of snow photography looks like: big, fluffy, slow-falling flakes that
stand out perfectly against the background rather than turning to a
streak like rain or sleet.

sure you apply an overexposure of somewhere
between +1 and +2 stops; you want the histogram to
be touching the extreme right, thereby ensuring the
snow is actually white while retaining its inherent
texture. Most falling snow will record, like rain, as
streaks or lines on the background, but occasionally
the right sort of snow for photography can occur
– big individual flakes falling slowly with little wind
to blow them around. In these conditions they will
appear as distinct flakes at most shutter speeds that
aren't too slow.

A final consideration in extreme or cold conditions like this is battery life. Modern batteries are
surprisingly long-lasting, but keeping a spare in your
inside pocket will give it every chance of holding its
charge or even restoring a little to one that has given
up in the low temperatures.

PREPARE A SUBMISSION TO A SPECIALIST IMAGE LIBRARY

Over the course of the last few years, and pretty much running parallel to the massive uptake of digital SLRs and interest in photographing the natural world, there has been a far greater increase in the supply of images for potential purchase than there has demand. While this has meant that the returns per individual image have reduced, the fact remains that stepping into the organized world of selling your images offers not only the chance to help towards funding the cost of your hobby, but also acts as a benchmark as to where you are in terms of general standard. The disciplines that image libraries can impose on any submissions are also a good way to ensure you really get to grips with the file management and processing side of things, too, as covered in Chapter 9.

There are a number of different types of image library and it pays to progress slowly through the hierarchy of these, accepting the fact that in the early stages sales and returns will be low. The process is partly about acquiring the discipline to prepare submissions.

The easiest arena in which to start selling is through one of the so-called microstock agencies. These are classic high-volume, low-value royalty-free agencies (*see* box), such as Shutterstock and BigStockPhoto. Bird images are a tiny fraction of what they have to offer their clients, but they do need them so they can be a good place to start. If you feel intrinsically uncomfortable with this sort of model (and once an image is royalty-free there is no turning), you could try another generalist agency that actually offers the chance to decide on an image-by-image basis what sort of route you wish to take to market it, and that is Alamy.

For all of these image libraries the technical quality of the image (dust free, correct file size, correct

RIGHTS MANAGED OR ROYALTY FREE?

There are two main bases on which images are sold, and each determine the rights the customer is purchasing in terms of the image's use.

With a 'rights managed' image the end-user is effectively paying a fee for each and every use of the image – in other words, paying every time they use it. It may be that they pay a price that has various defined uses built in, but the scope and extent will always be pre-arranged, agreed and priced accordingly. This should realize the highest fees for the photographer, but obviously the images have to have a certain uniqueness or impact to justify their cost. Some images can demand and receive an additional premium here in terms of exclusivity.

For a 'royalty-free' image the end-user pays a one-off fee that allows them multiple uses in multiple media within the terms of the licence they have purchased, which may cover a geographical area or a time period. There is no scope for exclusive arrangements and it is a volume-driven arena in which to operate.

exposure, suitably sharp and in focus, and so on) is the main criteria on which they accept new material rather than artistic merit per se or even uniqueness of image. It is important you go into potential supply agreements with them with your eyes wide open as to the nature of this marketplace, especially if you think you have something unique or special image-wise. Type 'Puffin' into the search engine of any of these libraries and several thousand images appear for the buyer to choose from!

As the quality, depth and breadth of your portfolio grows, being taken on by one of the specialist natural history image libraries (such as Nature

▶ Fig. 6.11
There are over 12,000 images
with the keyword "Puffin" in
their details on the generalist
image library Alamy's website
– hard to make yours stand
out, but still a good place to
learn about preparing work
for an image library.

▶ Fig. 6.12
There are only just under 850
Puffin images on specialist
natural history image library
FLPA's website – easier to
stand out perhaps, but the
standard is much higher and
it's a hard hurdle to climb to
get libraries like this to take
on your work. You'll need
something different from
Puffins in your portfolio, too.

Picture Library, FLPA and RSPB Images) is a realistic
goal or target to set yourself. Again, don't expect to
get rich in the process – it takes many years to build
up a critical mass with any library anyway – but as
a measure of where you are and for a great sense of
achievement if you are taken on, it is very much recommended. These agencies select new contributors
very much based on the quality of their work from a
creative as well as technical perspective, the diversity
of their portfolio and its potential to complement
rather than replicate the subjects, images and
photographers they work with already; it's not an
easy step to make these days.

USE OF THE INTERNET: PHOTO-SHARING, WEBSITES AND FORUMS

In much the same way that digital imaging has changed the whole nature of photography itself, the internet has changed the way photographers can share, present and critique their work and the work of others. One of the undoubted downsides of digital photography is the vast number of images that never see the light of day – they end up on hard drives unprinted and often unseen. If your photography is simply for your own pleasure then there is, of course, nothing wrong with this, but if you want to share or promote your work the internet is an easy environment in which to do so, although it does come with some obvious notes of caution.

Photo Sharing

An easy starting point is an imaging-sharing service such as Flickr. At the time of writing they were offering 1TB of free storage for anyone joining up with them, which at the resolution required for internet display is a huge number of images. Once enrolled you can easily upload your images, each of which will have its own weblink created within your gallery,

making the whole process of sending simple links to people very simple and straightforward. From here it's also very easy to link images across to any social media platform you might be a regular user of, such as Facebook.

Facebook of course also offers the opportunity to upload and share your images, and its very nature means that they will automatically be flagged to any of your friends in that environment. It is worth noting that any images uploaded onto Facebook go through a fairly brutal resizing process and often end up looking very jagged and over-sharpened, which doesn't always do them justice. At the same time all the EXIF data inside the file (which should contain all your copyright details) is routinely wiped out, thereby removing any direct linkage with you as the taker of the image (and therefore the copyright owner). If they are images that you want to keep track of or have some commercial value you can overcome this by simply adding a watermark using your photo processing software.

Images uploaded to Flickr do not undergo this data removal process and it is also able to accommodate much higher resolution images, which will do them far greater justice. One offers a gallery, the other an instant sharing process, so it's horses for courses and it will depend on which you prefer.

◀ Fig. 6.13
Sites like Flickr and 500px are good for sharing your work with others and making it easy to see in one place. They are for all genres of photography, though; there are filters to drill down to natural history-type images only.

Websites

Pick up pretty much any photography magazine (and there are plenty of them to choose from these days) and you'll easily find a company or two offering you the chance to have your own website. It used to be that all these offered were some very basic templates and it was still quite complicated to finesse the design, upload images and organize galleries, but this is a marketplace that has grown exponentially in recent times, so now they will help you get a domain name (or website address), offer a far greater range of flexibility in terms of look and feel and also functionality of the site, speedy and bulk uploading of your images, and good amounts of free storage at very reasonable monthly or annual rates. The majority of them also offer the opportunity to sell your images either as downloadable files or as prints which you supply, using the likes of PayPal for financial transactions.

Once you have a portfolio of which you are justifiably proud there is little doubt that having your own website is an ideal way to show it to the world; if you have any serious aspirations in this area it is probably essential to do so. Key to its success, though, is to make sure that it's easy to navigate for the visitor, looks good on mobile devices/tablets (check with the supplier how they handle this in their underlying software) and that you keep content fairly fresh and up to date – nothing looks worse that revisiting a website and seeing 'latest news' that is six months old! It is also worth checking with the service provider what protection they have against 'right-clicking' on the images on the site to prevent people from easily downloading your work. If they have protection here (and many do), it will reduce the need to plaster the images with copyright notices.

Internet Forums

The role of bird-watching forums when it comes to looking for rarer species or unusual sightings close to home has already been covered, but similar forums also exist when it comes to sharing your images. Many of these are generic in their nature (for example 500px) but the well-developed ones will have nature or wildlife-related sub-forums or categories for you to drill down to. There are specialist ones as well, such as naturephotographers.net.

The upsides of sharing your work here, as well as viewing and commenting on others, are obvious: the chance to get feedback and critique on your work, the chance to learn by looking at other enthusiasts' work (especially if they are at the same learning stage as you) and quite possibly the chance to find fellow enthusiasts with whom you might be able to meet up and photograph alongside. In sport it is often said that playing against an opponent who is better than you helps you improve most rapidly, and the same can be said of photography. Finding fellow enthusiasts you can learn and share with can only be a positive thing, and in this respect internet forums are a modern extension of the massive network of Camera Clubs to be found around the country. Clubs don't appeal to everyone and while many do have very good nature sections they tend to be more generalist in nature and approach (and understandably so), so forums do offer a focused (and more regular) alternative.

As with all things internet-related, forums do come with a health warning. Be prepared to be thick-skinned at times, and if you want more feedback than 'Nice pic' make sure you contribute by commenting constructively on other people's work as well. It is also good practice in this environment not to share sites you have been photographing at, especially during breeding season.

◀ **Figs 6.14a and 6.14b**
Template-based, easy to
upload to and requiring
relatively little IT and
no coding skills, service
providers like the US-
based Photoshelter offer a
reasonably easy first step to
having your own website,
when you feel you have a
broad enough portfolio and
will be able to keep it updated
regularly. The alternative is
a blog-based site using a
set-up like Wordpress – text
accompanied by images in
single article/feature-type
entries is what this kind of
service provider offers.

Some Creative Approaches

USE OF SHUTTER SPEED

Look at many landscape images, particularly those involving water, and you will see that many creative effects and styles have been achieved by using slow shutter speeds. We have already seen how helpful it is in terms of ensuring image sharpness to look for as fast a shutter speed as possible; however, varying the shutter speed is one of the key ways to introduce some variety and creativity into your images. It is important to make sure you adopt good practice when doing so, though, especially with long lenses (*see* box).

Varying shutter speeds will affect the way that the movement in your image is captured, so this is a thought process that applies mainly, but certainly not exclusively, to the genre of flight photography.

SLOW SHUTTER SPEED 'MUSTS'

When using slow shutter speeds for creative effect, or even just because the light levels are low and dictate it, it is important to avoid the dreaded camera shakes. Given that you are likely to be using a long focal length of lens that will exaggerate this problem even more, here are a few simple must-do things to remember:

- Make absolutely sure that everything on your tripod and tripod head is fully tightened; a wobbly leg or loose mount can ruin the image unknowingly. If you have rotated your lens using the lens collar, double check this is tight too.
- Use a cable release rather than pressing the shutter. If this isn't possible or practical (you might not have the time to rummage through your bag), switch your camera to a two-second or ten-second timer release mode, which will achieve the same 'hands off' benefit when the shutter opens.

- Set your camera mirror to 'mirror lockup'. This can be activated through your camera's menu or custom functions. It has the effect of lifting the mirror out of the way so that when the shutter is released the internal movements in the camera are minimized.
- If you have image stabilization on your lens it can sometimes pay to switch it off. Its vibrations can have an additional impact through particularly long exposures.
- Remember that to get slow shutter speeds in normal light conditions you will need to go for a low ISO (down to 100 if you can) and then almost certainly close down the aperture, which will increase the depth of field; bear this in mind when you arrange your composition.

◀ Fig. 7.1
Dalmatian Pelican *Pelecanus crispus* in breeding plumage photographed in northern Greece. Canon 1d Mk4, 500mm, ƒ5.6, 1/640sec, ISO 400.

▲ Fig. 7.2
Fast shutter speeds (this was 1/2500sec) are required to really freeze motion, such as this Sandhill Crane *Grus Canadensis* in flight.

For sharp images here it is desirable to use a shutter speed of 1/1,000sec – or faster, if possible – as this will significantly increase your success rate over even 1/500sec.

A sharp, frozen bird in flight, however, can look a little artificial at times. A little like images of a helicopter with frozen propellers, it just doesn't feel right. As a consequence, once you have got to grips with the challenges of panning and focusing, you might want to gradually reduce the shutter speed so that, while the key elements of the bird remain sharp (the head in particular), the wings are recorded with a degree of motion blur that will convey the sense of movement and effort that is being put into the flying process. Just what shutter speed will be needed for this will depend on an array of different factors, including how good the light is, but it is mostly determined by the size of bird – bigger birds with slower wing beats require generally slower shutter speeds to freeze than smaller birds with much faster wing beats.

▲ Fig. 7.3
Although the head of this Razorbill *Alca torda* is sharp, even a
shutter speed of 1/1600sec is not quite fast enough to prevent some
movement showing in the wings of the bird. It does give a greater
sense of motion, though, with the slightly blurred effect.

▲ Fig. 7.4
This group of Knot *Calidris canutus* blasting off from their high tide
roost at Snettisham on the Wash works well thanks to a couple of
key elements. Firstly, the shutter speed is ideally balanced to render
a high sense of motion in the vast majority of birds but give clear
identity to the species and what is happening by virtue of the fact
that a number of individual birds are still clear and sharp. Secondly,
their incredible density (there are literally no gaps) and the frame-
filling impact add a sense of scale of what's taking place in front of
the lens.

Of course, not all flight shots involve individual
birds. Many species are more normally found flying
in flocks, with some of the large wader flocks or
starlings gathering to roost at night in the winter
months. Experimentation with shutter speed when
photographing large groups of birds on the move
can create some really dramatic images and there
is scope for plenty of creative interpretation as well

– not always to everyone's taste but, if you consider
your photography to be an art form rather than
purely capturing what you see, this is great territory
in which to make such a statement.

Although shutter speeds around 1/60sec and
1/125sec will be perfect for creating a sense of
movement, as in the image of Knot taking off in
Fig. 7.4 (while making sure the background provides

▲ Fig. 7.5
This extreme slow-shutter speed image of a large flock of Snow
Geese *Chen caerulescens* taking off from a field at last light is
extremely impressionistic in nature. The trees can just be seen
through the thinner layer of birds at the top of the image, before
the main group leaving the ground comes up to join them. There is
just enough definition to see what they are but the rest is left to the
imagination and interpretation of the viewer; it's photography as art
perhaps and not everyone's cup of tea.

a contrast to the predominant colour of the species
in question), an even slower shutter speed such
as 1/15sec can create some ghostly shapes and
movement patterns as large groups take to the air.
Look here to have something in the image that can
remain sharp if you can (a feature in the landscape,
for instance) – the contrast between the extreme
blur of the moving birds and a sharp permanent
object will increase the visual impact.

When undertaking this type of experimental
photography, you need to accept that a high percentage of your images will not have any appeal at
all. They simply won't work if there's too much blur
and not enough shape, form or definition to create a
recognizable scene. To a certain extent that is part of
the attraction – you are only partially in control, for a
change, but sticking with it can give some extraor-
dinary results, and at least in the digital age it costs

▲ Fig. 7.6
This image of one of the magnificent Gannet *Sula bassana* colonies to be found at Hermaness on Unst is also an extreme slow-shutter speed interpretation. The result is not only the landscape photographer's desire for increased spread of the surf pounding on the rocks below, but also for any soaring birds flying through the scene to appear as a streaked line.

nothing but your own review time to delete the ones that didn't work.

There are further experiments you can try with a slow shutter speed and an individual bird. Conventional panning with a slow shutter speed can increase the sense of speed and movement; but try deliberately reversing the pan while using a slow shutter speed and some unusual smoke trail effects can appear behind the birds. Again, the percentage of success here is low, but get it right and the impact is undeniable; it's a fun process to spend time working on, too.

▲ Fig. 7.7
This is another creative use of shutter speed involving Snow Geese
Chen caerulescens. The camera was pulled back in a sort of reverse
panning while the shutter was being pressed to create these smoke
trails.

Working with slow shutter speeds doesn't have to
be confined to moving birds. There will be occasions
where the bird can be the static element in the image and something else can have its nature changed
through the creative use of slower shutter speeds
– blurring, moving water such as a weir or waterfall,
for instance. Here you are looking for as static a
subject as you can find and just hoping it stands still
for a reasonable amount of time – enough to get at
least one sharp shot in the sequence!

Don't think of slow shutter speeds exclusively as
a way of photographing birds in flight. Many birds
ruse or shake their wings to clean their feathers and
this can provide an opportunity to record the movement as more of a blur. Always remember to look for
something in the image that has a static element,
though.

▲ Fig. 7.8
It took several images before achieving one where this winter plumage Black-headed Gull *Larus ridibundus* stood perfectly still throughout the 1/13sec exposure required to add some blur to the weir it was standing on.

▶ Fig. 7.9
The in-focus branch on which this Pygmy Cormorant *Phalacrocorax pygmeus*, photographed in Hungary, is standing is key to making this shot work; it remains sharp and in focus while the back-lit bird, recently landed there, shakes itself dry.

IMPORTANCE OF PERSPECTIVE – GET LOW!

One of the most frustrating aspects of the vast majority of bird observation hides situated around the UK's reserves is that they do not allow you to get yourself at the same height relative to the ground as your subject. This is a vital element to achieving intimate and creative bird photography; nothing is more impactful than being at eye-level, and conversely nothing looks less so than an image taken from a steep downwards angle. At times, of course, it is the only option and, when it is, working with a long lens on subjects that are a reasonable distance away from you will lessen the perceived heights involved. When, however, you are in your own hide (*see* Chapter 8), trying to work at equal height to your bird is key, and when this involves photographing birds on the ground or in the water it adds a whole new dynamic and scope for creativity as well.

▼ Fig. 7.10

The intimacy of this portrait of a Sanderling *Calidris alba* on a tidal beach is achieved solely by the low angle achieved by lying on the sand waiting for him to feed his way towards me.

▲ Fig. 7.11
The extreme blur at the bottom of this image of an Arctic Skua *Stercorarius parasiticus* is achieved solely by lying down in the grassy meadow he was sitting in and photographing through some of the grass between the front of the 500mm lens used and the bird itself, while having a small depth of field of *f*4.

▲ Fig. 7.12
Here the 'mush' at the bottom of this portrait of a Guillemot *Uria aalge* introduces a new colour element into the image, provided by some pink thrift on the grassy cliff top.

Once you are at ground level, then literally every inch lower you can go will help to increase the drama. This position will also introduce 'mush' to the bottom of your images, providing there is vegetation on the ground between yourself and your subject. 'Mush' is certainly not a technical term, but it pretty much describes the de-focused colour-wash effect that foreground foliage has. In an ideal world the colour of your 'mush' will be the same as your background and the result will be a subject (or partially visible subject) that appears to float in a sea of colour all around. If the foreground and background don't match colour-wise, give some consideration to

the line where the colour changes and where you want it to be. It will have to go through your subject somewhere, so try to make it as non-distracting as possible.

If it's grass you are photographing through (as in the majority of instances), just be sure to avoid getting so absorbed in what you are doing that you miss one tall blade or stem that is between you and your subject but close to it; it will show as a distinct line in your image and become an obstruction rather than a creative effect or style.

It doesn't have to be grass, though. If the distances between yourself and a rock and a rock and your

◀ Fig. 7.13
My 500mm lens was a matter of inches above the water level to capture this extreme low-level view of this beautiful Black-necked Grebe *Podiceps nigricollis* in the Netherlands. My tripod was in the water too, as was I, and I needed a right-angle viewfinder to see through the lens.

◀ Fig. 7.14
This young Mute Swan *Cygnus olor* became so curious by my presence in my local canal that he would swim too close, almost putting his head inside the lens hood of my 500mm lens!

subject are reasonably significant, the rock can also be used to create the same de-focused foreground effect. This can particularly useful as an approach when working with seabirds or shorebirds generally. It is often quite difficult to get 'different'-looking images or sometimes even a clear view of them.

The benefit of getting low also applies when working with water birds. Every inch closer to the water you can get, the more impactful the image, the more mirror-like the water and the deeper the reflection of the subject. This allows you to place the bird more towards the top of the frame to really emphasize the reflection and give an even greater sense of actually being in the water with it.

This may very often actually need to be the case as it is only by getting your lens to a matter of inches above the water that you can achieve the effect shown in the image of the Black-necked Grebe (Fig. 7.13). There are obvious risks to getting into the water like this, especially when it comes to looking after your kit, and there are two different approaches. The simplest (and if the birds in question are habituated enough to people) is to place your tripod into the water, leaving the head and top of the legs standing proud, onto which you attach your lens. If you are close to the bank when you do this you may be able to lie there and use a right-angle viewfinder to look through. The alternative involves putting on chest waders (neoprene ones are the warmest and driest without doubt) and sitting in the water behind the camera. The right-angle viewfinder will still be required here as without it you'd have to have your face in the water to get your eye level with the viewfinder! The need for caution when attaching and removing your kit from the tripod goes without saying, and it is definitely worth locking the vertical movement of your tripod head tight so that you don't accidentally lower your lens into the water while you are absorbed in what you are photographing!

The alternative to simply sitting in the water like this, and necessary when the subjects are more wary or are not going to approach your side of the water, is to use a floating hide. These are covered in more detail in Chapter 8.

USING A WIDE-ANGLE/REMOTE

The vast majority of bird photography, as we have seen, involves the use of long lenses. On the whole this is based on reasons of practicality; most species are not confiding enough to allow you close enough to work at short distances, and even a well established hide has a circle of closeness around it, especially with the noise of a shutter going off resonating from it. There are of course exceptions to this rule, such as Puffins, and here common sense must prevail in terms of working with them. Approach them low along the ground, slowly working your way into position, and – given that they tend to be found on cliff tops – taking great care where you are

▶ Fig. 7.15
I chose to use a wide-angle lens (24–70mm) to place this murmuration of Starlings *Sturnus vulgaris* in the setting of the fields they were gathering together in, before they dropped as one into the conifer copse where they would roost that night.

▲ Fig. 7.16
The camera and wide angle lens (24–70mm) I used to create this close-up image of Robin *Erithacus rubecula* in the snow was fired using a remote wireless device to fire the shutter. I had pre-focused at a spot where I had anticipated the bird being in the frame.

going and paying attention to the general stability of the area. Before you approach, spend some time watching the bird to make sure that you are not blocking access to the burrows if it is breeding. There are plenty of non-breeders in most Puffin colonies, but observation time will ensure you've picked the right one.

Compositionally, the effect that you are looking for here is a dominant subject (which the wide-angle lens will ensure) but a clear sense of habitat and setting, too. Have this in mind as you work your way into position, thinking also about the direction of the light at all times.

However, in the majority of instances you won't be able to be anywhere near your subject when it comes to achieving this style of image and you will

need to work on a remote basis. Until recently, this involved the creation of very long cables attached to your shutter release cable, but there is now a plethora of infrared trigger devices available, even infrared trigger devices that fire the camera when a beam is broken. The latter is of more use with mammal photography given the size of birds, but using a remote trigger to fire your camera when you are some distance away from it opens up an array of creative possibilities.

When setting up for this, the camera needs to be stable – either on a tripod/stand or on the ground. It is also a good idea to have some sort of soundproofing around it so that the noise of the shutter is reduced. In fact, this is more likely to be the mirror going up before the shutter fires, with the result that the bird is hopping out of the scene in most of your images. Depending on the set-up and the sensitivity of the species in question, choose between either a thick camouflage rain cover at a basic level or a home-made soundproof box at a more sophisticated level. For the latter, plywood will be fine, then add some foam rubber on the inside to soak up the sound. Leave the back panel as removable so that you can get the camera in and out easily and also so that once it is in position you can look through the viewfinder to set up your composition and focusing. You should look to manually focus, as you can't be certain where the bird will be in the frame, making autofocus unreliable. You will also likely need a smallish aperture of ƒ8 or ƒ11 to increase your

chances of the bird being sharp in the image, too; set up in aperture priority to allow for changing light conditions through the day.

The subjects that work best with this approach are those that you are certain will regularly visit a particular feeding spot or landing perch that you have set up. The same principles covered in working at nest sites then apply (*see* Chapter 8) when it comes to establishing the camera's presence. This again is a randomly successful process and you need patience and self-discipline to not keep popping to the camera and checking how it is going: see it instead as a longer term exercise with new things to learn every day.

▶ Fig. 7.17
This Coot *Fulica atra* was photographed early in the morning and is typical of how backlighting works – a dark background emphasizing the rim of light that forms around the subject when the sun is low in the sky and coming from behind. It gives more of a sense of mood and atmosphere than a conventionally lit image.

▲ Fig. 7.18
Photographing this backlit Puffin *Fratercula arctica* lets the light
shine through its colourful summer beak and also any sandeels it
may have in its beak as it returns to feed its young.

CREATIVE USE OF BACKLIGHTING

The principles of backlighting, where the light is
coming from the rear of the subject, have been
covered in an earlier chapter. Working with this form
of lighting will introduce a real sense of mood to
your images.

The light needs to be low in the sky to consider
backlit images, so this is very much an early morning or late evening approach. Misty, early morning
conditions around water work particularly well (the
mist will diffuse the sun, allowing you to shoot for a
little longer) and also dark backgrounds which allow

the rim lighting or halo effect around your subject
to really stand out. Sometimes the light can actually
shine through your subject, too, as in raised wings,
the colourful beak of a Puffin or the sandeels in their
beaks. The motto here is to keep your eyes open for
opportunities and apply this approach in different
circumstances.

One word of caution, though, and that is to
beware of lens flare caused when light entering the
lens reflects off the lens elements. To avoid this,
always use a lens hood (the deeper the better) or if
necessary hold your hand in front of and above the
top of the lens to block the directional light. Make
sure your lens is clear of dirt particles, too, as they
can cause the same effect.

▲ Fig. 7.19
This pair of nesting White Storks *Ciconia ciconia* is a good example of how a distinctive shape and context can make a silhouetted image still instantly recognizable as well as impactful.

SHOOTING FOR SILHOUETTES

Silhouettes are images in their simplest state: a background of colour and the defined black shape of the subject in front of it. They certainly don't fall into the classic record-keeping category of photography as there is no detail in the subject to see, but with the right selection of subject and setting it should still be identifiable otherwise the image won't work in the way it should. It is important, therefore, to pick subjects with a degree of distinctiveness about their shape or the setting in which they are positioned – the shape alone has to tell the story of the image.

After the distinctive shape, the next key ingredient is colour and this depends on the sky doing its bit – it also means that you will be looking for these sorts of images at sunrise or sunset. It often helps here to have a little bit of cloud on the scene as it reflects the setting sun from underneath and adds some textural variety as well as colour intensity to the background. If you really want to intensify these orange colours you can pre-set your white balance to a high setting such as 7000 or 8000 Kelvin ideally at the point of capture, although you can also adjust this in your RAW processing.

When it comes to ensuring you get the correct exposure, it is worth remembering that you are in effect looking to expose correctly for the sky and

▲ Figs 7.20a and 7.20b
Both these silhouettes are of Sandhill Crane *Grus Canadensis.* The first is photographed at sunrise when the sky had lots of colour, the second on a cool cloudless evening when there was no colour other than the paling blue of the sky, emphasized by a cool white balance setting.

▲ Fig. 7.21
Here the colour surrounding this Redshank *Tringa totanus* as he moved through the shallow waters was caused by the after sunset glow of the cloud base created after the volcanic eruption in Iceland in 2010 – even though the image was taken in the Netherlands!

render the subject black. Using exposure compensation in the methodology described earlier, start at around -1 in terms of compensation and keep on going until you have a clear black spike on your histogram to represent the subject and an intense and strong background colour.

There doesn't always have to be an orange sky as a background. Cool, clear blue skies at around the same time of day (and especially if there are a few pink fluffy clouds to add to the equation) will work just as well. Remember, however, to take your white balance in the opposite direction (around 4000K or so) to emphasize the blue.

Sometimes the intense colours in the sky can be reflected in the water. When there is no wind and the mirror-like water is full of colour, this offers

another opportunity to try the same approach.

A final word of warning here – always avoid looking directly at the sun through your camera and lens. It becomes less risky to do so as it approaches the horizon and if there is a veil of cloud in front of it, but your lens will magnify its intensity and can cause damage to your eyes.

SMALL IN FRAME – LET THE LANDSCAPE TELL THE STORY

When you have bought a long (and expensive) lens it's very tempting to want to use it to its maximum effect and fill the frame up as much as possible with your subject. The need to allow your subject room to breathe has been covered earlier, but the setting is often as important as the subject and on many

▲ Fig. 7.22
It is the intense blues along with the shape and form of the section of iceberg this Fulmar *Fulmarus glacialis* is sitting in front of, and how it dominates the bird in terms of scale, that add the impact to this image.

occasions representing the subject as simply a small element in the final image can tell a much more powerful story than a close-up ever can.

For this sort of image to work it is important that the setting itself conveys a sense of scale or is providing the drama almost in its own right. If this isn't the case there is a danger that the photo simply looks like you weren't able to get close enough to the subject to take the image you would have liked to. Heavy precipitation, whether in the form of rain or snow, is a classic example of this. A scene full of falling rain with a small bird braving it out tells a powerful story, as does a small bird walking through a large expanse of water. Put a small bird in the middle of a clutter of branches, though, and the drama just isn't there.

BLACK AND WHITE

Although modern SLR cameras are able to capture and present colour in a phenomenal amount of detail and unerring accuracy (high-end cameras are capable of representing more than an already staggering 16,000 different colour tones), there is still something about a high contrast black-and-white image that can capture the imagination. There are many features, not just to birds themselves but the context and surroundings in which we see them, that stunning colour can obscure – texture, form and shape being the holy trinity for black-and-white photographers.

What black-and-white images allow us to see and appreciate is tonal range. Within the 16,000+ colour tones each pixel may be able to create, several thousand of those will just be what you might generically describe as green. Look carefully at any tree in leaf, however, and although the leaves may be green there are shades and variations galore and this is what black-and-white, or monochrome, photography allows us to appreciate. Seeing the world this way gives us a greater appreciation of tone, which will be of help and benefit when it comes to colour work.

Although your camera may well have a mono-chrome setting, take any images you may wish to consider as monochrome reproductions in your normal colour mode and convert them to black and white at the processing stage. This will give you far greater control over the subtleties of the conversion, rather than simply desaturating the image.

▲ Fig. 7.24
This Guillemot *Uria aalge*, already essentially a black and white bird, was an ideal monochrome subject on a white cliff in front of a dark cave.

The sorts of images of birds that work well are silhouettes and other high contrast situations. Fluffy clouds in a blue-sky setting will also add some real punch, as will a setting where the subject is in sun-light but there are areas of shade or darkness around to provide real tonal contrast.

◀ Fig. 7.23
Bittern *Botaurus stelaris* are shy birds of the reedbed, more often heard than seen, so allowing this individual to be dominated in the image by the towering reeds as he feeds along the edge tells a very appropriate story.

ADD DEPTH USING OUT-OF-FOCUS ELEMENTS

This is a simple but effective way of adding a greater sense of depth and an almost 3D quality to your images, and works at its best when you are photographing birds that live in a group or colony setting. Don't look for a perfectly clear view of your subject – rather, you want to be photographing past one in front of your main target or have one or more behind or to one side of it. Working with a long lens will always compress perspective and, providing there is some distinct shape, form and colour to the object (it doesn't have to be another bird necessarily, just distinctive and recognizable even when it's out of focus), having a layer of subject clean and sharp and another layer de-focused will instantly add an additional dimension to your image. This is very much one of those occasions when you have to 'see' the picture; it won't happen by accident. When you are working on an individual bird and are having to work hard to get a clean background because of the presence of other birds, remember this type of image as it will be the best time to try it out. Then it becomes a question of not just watching and wait-ing for the main subject to move to the exact pose you'd like, but at the same time looking at any others in the composition; it takes concentration but adds a different style to your work.

▲ Fig. 7.25
While watching for the pair of Little Auk *Alle alle* in the foreground to get their heads in complimentary positions, I was also watching the one in the out-of-focus background to ensure it too was composed correctly in terms of body position and how it was holding its head so that the image was balanced.

TIME-LAPSE

Strictly speaking, all that a video or movie sequence is, is a series of still images replayed at a very fast reproduction rate so that you don't see the joins. The production of time-lapse sequences of individual images works on precisely the same principle and if

you are looking to jazz up a website or have another element to any talks or slideshows that you may be doing, a short time-lapse sequence can add to that mix.

The basic set-up for this is to position your camera in a stable setting, such as your tripod, so that it doesn't move during the entire time of photographing. It's probably best to set your camera using aperture priority mode so that it can change settings with any change of light, but if you want to emphasize the changing light conditions of a sun-rise or sunset you might prefer a manual approach. Manually focus the camera to avoid the focal point hopping around during the sequence. It is then a question of taking an image approximately every five, ten or twenty seconds, depending on what you are recording.

Medium or large JPEGs will be perfectly adequate here and will avoid an enormous amount of processing time converting from RAW files very similar images. You will need a great deal of them – every second of video playback will need around thirty frames and even for a fifteen-second end product you will need 450 images; if you take one at ten-second intervals, say, that will still take an hour-and-a-quarter's photography to capture. Depending on your camera, you will either be able to set it directly through the menu or use a programmable cable release to take images at the regularity you decide, while you get on with some other photography or enjoy a cup of tea from your flask!

Clearly for most bird species this sort of end product is impractical, but mass groups of birds such as geese arriving or leaving a roosting location, or seabird colonies where there is constant movement on the ground and in the air, both offer the opportunity to experiment with this different approach. When it comes to processing the images they will need dropping into a movie-making software program such as iMovie or Movie Maker.

PARTIAL SUBJECT VISIBILITY

A lot has been discussed about the need to 'see' an image, but sometimes the opportunity to capture a moment and convey the personality of a species can be seized when it is trying to see *you*. The whole of your subject need not necessarily be in view to capture its character; sometimes the cheeky peek round a tree stump or look above a rock will say much more than a fully visible subject. These are images that you can't really set up for; you just have

to spot them and press the button, making sure you leave plenty of space for where the subject is likely to be looking in the context of the setting.

▲ Fig. 7.26
It's the very fact that you can't see all of this Kittiwake *Rissa tridactyla* as it peers round the side of the cliff ledge that it is nesting on that provides the intimacy of the image – it's almost as if it is seeking you out as you look at it.

Chapter 8

The Importance of Fieldcraft

When you first get started trying to take pictures of birds, even with a long telephoto lens it soon becomes apparent that just having the kit itself is no guarantee of anything. The vast majority of wild birds are not that straightforward in terms of getting close to them, and even though a 500mm lens might look like it could give you close-up images of the craters on the moon the reality is that, even for common and easily approachable birds in the garden, to get frame-filling images you need to be around five metres away. It's clear, therefore, that not only is a great deal of patience required, but also the knowledge and skill set that is best summarized as fieldcraft.

KNOW WHAT'S HAPPENING AND WHEN (SEASONS, MIGRATION, ETC.)

In Chapter 5 a number of initial projects to get you started were covered, including simple or complex set-ups in your garden, visiting reserves and attending organized workshops. Whichever of these you may decide to begin with, there is an important step that you need to have undertaken before all that, and it's ensuring you have a better than basic understanding of birds and how they live their lives.

Many people come into bird photography from a bird-watching background so this will be a step that can be gone through instantaneously, but for those that haven't then some time spent researching and reading about birds generally is essential. You really do need to know simple things, such as which species are resident and which migratory, when the latter are likely to be here (are they summer visitors or winter ones?), which habitats they are likely to be found in, and so on. You might be aware that Ospreys are a highlight of the Cairngorms National Park in Scotland, but there is no point heading there in winter hoping to photograph them as they will be in North Africa at that time of the year; in southern UK though you may very well find one heading north in the spring or back south in late summer on their migration. In the same vein, heading to a WWT reserve such as Caerlaverock to photograph Whooper Swans and Barnacle Geese will be a pointless exercise in July as they will be in Iceland and Svalbard respectively.

Understanding when birds breed, where they might do so, how and when they migrate from one part of the world or even just from one habitat to another (Golden Plover and Dunlin, for instance, breed in the upland moors in the UK during the summer months then spend the winters feeding, generally in large flocks, around our coastlines) is essential to significantly increase your chances of looking in the right place at the right time for subjects to work with.

It also helps to understand the different migration routes and when the weather conditions are likely to have the best impact in terms of creating opportunities. Spring and autumn migrations see large numbers of birds gathering up for the 'safety in numbers' approach to their travels, which can lead to great concentrations as well as rare vagrants passing through. Locations such as the Scilly Isles and North Norfolk in the UK, and the Straits of Gibraltar

◀ Fig. 8.1
Goshawk *Accipiter gentilis* photographed in the Balkan mountains in Bulgaria. Canon 40D, 500mm + 1.4x converter, ƒ6.3, 1/800sec, ISO 200.

▲ Fig. 8.3
Golden Plover *Pluvialis apricaria* will be found in moorland habitats during the summer breeding months; in the winter they will feed on the estuary mudflats around the coast.

and the Bosphorus in southern Europe, trip off the tongue of keen birdwatchers; some simple research will tell you the best times to be at these places and what you might reasonably expect to see. In North Norfolk strong easterly winds are also usually a good lead in to both numbers and rarities being around; attention to detail and insight like this all helps increase your chances.

◀ Figs 8.2a and 8.2b
This group of Whooper Swan flying over a snow-covered Caerlaverock WWT reserve in winter **(a)** will almost all head to Iceland in the summer to breed, where this parent and cygnets **(b)** were photographed.

UNDERSTANDING YOUR SUBJECT – LEARN WHERE THEY GO AND WHY

The same practical knowledge and insight is equally essential when it comes to working with individual birds. You may well have all the identification and general behavioural knowledge about a particular species, but that won't necessarily get you close to the one you've found! The use of and issues associated with using your own hide will be covered in the next section, but before that it is important to decide where exactly you might want to place it and

▲ Fig. 8.4
Redwing *Turdus iliacus* are
drawn to hedgerows where
there are still good quantities
of berries to feed on; in
particularly cold Scandinavian
winters the numbers of birds
visiting the UK in search
of food like this increases
significantly.

▶ Fig. 8.5
Black-headed Gulls *Larus
ridibundus* are opportunist
feeders and will therefore
regularly gather at landfill
sites and recycling centres in
search of food.

that can only be decided on the basis of some initial observation of your species' behaviour and where it likes to go.

First of all, all birds need to feed and a high density of food in any location will prove an obvious attraction and quite possibly become a regular visiting spot. The simple peanut feeding pole in the garden bears testament to this. In the initial phases of finding species you need to look for natural sources of food that are attractive to birds. A dense crop of berries on roadside bushes in the winter will bring in Redwing and Fieldfare, the berry-laden rowan trees that dominate supermarket car parks are an instant attraction for resident thrushes and also Waxwing if it's a year when they are visiting in large numbers, a tractor ploughing or harrowing a field in the autumn will generally be followed by mixed Gull flocks which will remain when the work is over, and fish farms will draw in either resident or migratory Ospreys. All of these are locations and activities to store in your memory bank and be alert to when out and about, with or without your camera.

Once you have an understanding of what attracts birds food-wise you will be able to build up a map of possible places to visit in the appropriate season, and from there it is a relatively simple step to see if you can add to the attractiveness of a site in order to further concentrate the birds to a specific area and then photograph them. For garden and woodland birds this involves the sort of feeding station set-up described in Chapter 5, but it also applies to other types of birds, too. Buzzards, Crows and other birds of prey can be lured to feed at carrion, especially during the harder months of winter. For larger birds of prey that might feed on the carcass of a large mammal such as a deer or sheep, the practicalities and legal issues relating to the disposal of dead livestock, along with the challenges of finding a suitable site and ensuring a regular supply of food to encourage reasonably regular visits, may be enough to put you off. (Birds of prey are among the wariest of bird types so this sort of work and set-up takes a great deal of time to establish, and any hide you want to use must have been established at the site for some time before you even think of getting there with a camera.)

For many smaller species road-kill victims such as rabbit work perfectly well, and there are many suppliers of day-old chicks for zoos, animal farms and bird of prey centres you can purchase from. When working with this type of food it is important

◄ Fig. 8.6
It took my Norwegian friend several winters before this Goshawk *Accipiter gentilis* would come to the re-created plucking post setting he had created for them in his nearby woods. I had to enter his hide in the dark and sit completely still until a bird came, and even then had to take images just one frame at a time to ensure it was not spooked by the moving camera or shutter.

▶ **Figs 8.7a and 8.7b**
This Linnet *Carduelis
cannabina* (**a**) and House
Martin *Delichon urbica*
(**b**) were drawn to these
muddy puddles for different
reasons – the former for a
drink (it was the only water
source in the area) and the
latter early in the summer to
collect mud for nest building.

to secure it well – tent pegs in a rabbit carcass will make it harder for foxes to drag it away at night or the Buzzard you are trying to photograph to grab it and fly off.

With dead fish being used as chum to attract Gannets off the back of boats or live minnows in a tray being used to attract Kingfishers to a perch, the extent to which the controlled and careful use of food can get you closer to your subject is significant,

and a long step on from childhood memories of taking a stale loaf of bread to the local duck pond. Some aspects of feeding, though, wander into moral, controversial and legal territories, especially when it comes to using live bait. Most people wouldn't think twice about using live mealworms to attract a Robin or Blackbird, but the aforementioned use of live fish to attract a Kingfisher, say, is too much for some but perfectly acceptable for others. Anything

◀ **Fig. 8.8**
This drinking Wood Pigeon
Columba palumbus was
taken at a drinking pool in
Hungary especially created
for bird photography.

warm-blooded is a line that very few would cross (using a live tethered pigeon, for example, to attract a large raptor) and there are well-established anti-cruelty laws here in the UK that prevent it anyway.

Birds need water as much as they need food, so regular watering holes, especially in dry summer seasons, are always going to attract them. Creating a small pool was covered in Chapter 5. If the water

▲ Fig. 8.9
The same drinking pool also acted as a bathing place for this Song
Thrush *Turdus philomelos*.

itself is the primary attraction rather than being used
as a mere prop, it's important that it is at least six
to eight inches deep so that the core temperature
doesn't get too high, otherwise birds will be put
off visiting. If this is not possible, it does need to
be cleaned and refilled almost daily in high temperatures and also cleaned regularly in the winter
months to prevent bacterial build-up. Deep pools
like this will need plenty of structural support, so
bear this in mind when embarking on building one.
That said, they do offer great photographic potential,
either for birds drinking on perches you may have
placed near them as they access the pool or when
they are splashing around while bathing.

Specific perches are not just used by birds as
approaches to food or water, though, and at the
beginning of the breeding season many male birds
will have regular perches that they like to use for
their territorial songs – either as a warning to other
males or to attract a female to pair and breed with.
The males will regularly work their way around their
territory, proclaiming their presence; once you've
seen this behaviour, it's another potential location to
set yourself up in and wait for the bird to return.

Birds are sometimes unable to be active for a
variety of reasons – during high tides in the case
of waders, when the mud they feed on is covered
by the sea; at night time for others such as Starling,

▲ Fig. 8.10
This Wren *Troglodytes troglodytes* would return to this foxglove to sing its head off every time it left the nearby nest, having delivered a beak full of insects to the young inside. I only needed to set up and wait for it to return every ten minutes or so

which also gather together in huge numbers for additional safety; or flocks of geese gathering in the middle of a lake or estuary. This roosting period is a regular gathering, a known behavioural pattern – and therefore a photographic opportunity. This can apply to small individual birds as well as large groups; many Tits, for instance, like to re-use nestboxes for a few extra degrees of warmth on winter nights.

Once you have discovered the telltale signs (in the form of droppings) of the latter or witnessed the former, it is simply a question of working out the light and time of day (tide or light related) that you need to be there again. Your expected and predicted behaviour might not always work out, but that's where patience is required as well as the self-motivation to keep coming back. If you've seen it happen there once, it will likely take more than one more visit to capture it in the right light again.

HIDES AND WORKING FROM THEM

For a great deal of photography the use of some form of hide is going to be essential. The scenarios already described in this chapter will have identified an array of opportunities with increased chances of birds returning based on good observational fieldwork. The hard bit is actually done at this point. Finding these opportunities takes what can appear to be large amounts of unproductive time; what follows is more a game of patience.

There is a range of models available when it comes to hides: from very portable, flat pop-up versions which are fine for a simple day visit to a location, to more rigid canvas structures either cube-shaped or the now more popular mini-dome-shaped variety. Whatever make you choose, and you'll need to decide that based on how long you think it will be in position, it must be sturdy and rigid so that it does not move in the wind (movement will deter birds approaching it – for the same reason, the openings or flaps should be able to be secured so they don't blow about). It should be dark inside (i.e. have a closable door) so that your presence in there does not show, and be able to accommodate you, your tripod and camera. If it is somewhere where you intend spending a long period of time (likely to be the case), make sure there's enough space for as comfortable a chair or stool as possible. As well as the access opening, there should be portholes for your lens and for viewing purposes, ideally on all three sides at a height that works from your seat, and if possible these should be able to conceal your presence behind the protruding lens hood as much as possible. Some of these do so by use of a conical lens port, but these are very restrictive in terms of seeing what's going on generally, so a flap of gauze or mesh hanging behind the opening will enable you to see through but still obscure your presence from outside.

It's possible to build semi-permanent hides for longer-term projects, too, and these can be made of plywood. In central Europe the use of one-way glass across the front of hides (*see* Fig. 8.12) can also give an amazing view of the setting and therefore what is approaching. The glass is reflective from the outside and presents itself as just more habitat for the birds approaching it; it therefore conforms to the 'dark inside' requirement outlined earlier. It does soak up a bit of light and needs to be of a high specification to avoid impacting on image clarity, but it really does give an amazing view.

A further variation on the hide theme is the floating hide. Usually home-made, this is a construction that involves either large polystyrene blocks or empty plastic barrels fitted in a U-shape with planks securely fitted to the top, onto which a small dome hide or similar is secured. Placing a beanbag on the planks to support the camera and lens and using a right-angle viewfinder given its closeness to the water level, the hide can then be manoeuvred slowly in shallow water while wearing chest waders. Keeping your feet on the bottom really is critical here or you will lose complete control. There are commercial variants of this that can be purchased too, but it's another example of just how your own inventiveness is the only constraint when it comes to creating a hide appropriate for a setting or opportunity.

It's a mistake to think that hides only work because they're camouflaged and blend into their surroundings. They are effective more because they are not the same shape and form as humans and birds do not associate them directly with the threat of people. Consequently one of the most effective forms of hide may actually be your car. Many species of bird frequent hedgerows and fields along roadsides, and it's even possible to find roads that run alongside estuaries and marshland where cars can act as perfect cover, since the recognizable human shape will not be visible to birdlife and birds will anyway be fairly habituated to the sight of cars. When using a car as a hide, a beanbag on an open

◀ Fig. 8.11
This pop-up hide, set up near a lek site in Norway, shows how a combination of camouflaged colouring and the lack of human shape allows a hide to work. An attempt at blending it into the surroundings by attaching a couple of conifer saplings on either front corner helps too.

◀ Fig. 8.12
This is a semi-permanent hide. Positioned at the edge of a muddy area in a wetland habitat in eastern Hungary, it is removable when the ground has dried out during summer. The area tends to attract spring migrant waders and terns, which will also have moved on by then, so there will be no disturbance.

◀ Fig. 8.13
This is a typical home-made floating hide – a canvas and camouflaged cover on a buoyant frame, being used in an area where the water is shallow enough to walk on the bottom of the lake.

window is the best form of support and, if you are planning a long stint, a sheet or towel to block out the light from the window behind you will remove any sign of your shape. Obviously you should only park in areas where you are not going to cause any inconvenience to other road users; make sure you remain aware of other cars if you decide you need to move location in a hurry. If you are driving slowly while looking for potential subjects and spot something, it can pay to switch the engine off and coast the last few metres up to it, having already stopped and prepared your kit and camera, so that the movement when you get in position is minimized. Again, take great care in terms of other road users.

There are clearly many ways in which to provide yourself with the cover of a hide and, as long as you follow common sense and good practice when it comes to not only putting them in place but also working from them, they are a key element in the bird photographer's armoury. Good practice is essential and you will also need to heed certain associated legal requirements with regard to nesting birds (*see next section*).

First and foremost, you must obtain permission from the landowner before you set any hide up, even in the remotest of locations. Ask yourself how you would explain yourself if he or she simply turned up while you were there and it will be clear why this is necessary, legal issues aside. Next, it makes sense to position your hide so that it is not obvious to any passer-by. You will be leaving it unattended for potentially several days or weeks and its presence will attract curiosity; it is not uncommon, sadly, to hear of hides being trashed, stolen or perches and feeders damaged.

When placing the hide, think ahead. Consider where the light is going to be coming from and move through as the day progresses, pre-visualize the images you are looking to achieve and position your hide accordingly, based on the size of the subject and the distance required by your lens and camera combination. With some wary species (and

▲ Fig. 8.14
A beanbag placed on a car door acts as perfect support for a long lens, while the car itself is an ideal hide that many birds will be used to seeing and not associate with people – providing you stay inside it. Note how hanging a coat over the far side windows ensures that you are blacked-out inside the car, thereby removing your distinctive shape.

especially if you are photographing at or near a nest site) you should try to introduce the hide to its final position in a series of stages; set it up a reasonable distance away from your end position and then watch to see if the birds' behaviour is being compromised at all. After a couple of days you can move it closer and then follow the same observational process until finally it is in the position where you want it and has been truly accepted. If at any point you have concerns then take it back a stage or accept that it's not a project that you can undertake this time. If you are working with a particularly sensitive species behaviourally it is also a good idea to point a dummy lens (a large plastic drinks bottle painted black or dark green) out of the front of the hide when

▲ Fig. 8.15
Golden Eagle *Aquila chrysaetos* can see a human approaching a potential feeding site with an overlooking hide from over two miles away and any association with people will stop them visiting the site. I had to enter this hide in Norway in the dark and leave in the dark to prevent this and I'll never forget when this female, my first ever Golden Eagle photographed, looked straight down the barrel of my lens at me.

you are not there; it ensures no change of shape when you are inside with a real lens pointing out, which must at this point have its own camouflage cover, too.

Depending on the species you are photographing, you may need to approach your hide in total darkness (and stay there until it is dark before you leave), so that the hide is never seen to have any association with people; raptors in particular require this. An alternative is to have an accomplice who walks to the hide with you, allowing you to get

settled, and then walks away, returning at a pre-agreed time (or better still after you have got in touch by text, assuming a mobile phone signal, and when there are no birds present) to repeat the operation and get you out. Birds watching from a distance will see the person and assume the coast is clear for them again.

Wherever you set up and whatever you do, though, the overriding principle must be that the birds' welfare is the number one priority. It is inevitable, even with good hide practice, that there will be some degree of disturbance caused. Your skill and judgement in understanding and recognizing when and if this is starting to impact on a bird's behaviour is imperative and, if you feel that this is the case, particularly in the breeding season, you should abandon the project and remove the hide.

NEST PHOTOGRAPHY: SOME DOS AND DON'TS

Until the advent of modern lightweight cameras most early bird photography was by necessity undertaken at the nest. This was also an age when there was an inherent fascination in nests and eggs that was considered acceptable in a way that it simply isn't today– and understandably so, given the dramatically increased pressures on our bird population.

There are now strict legal regulations in place when it comes to photographing at or near the nest sites of species of birds deemed to be most at risk. These are referred to as Schedule 1 species; an agreed maximum number of licences on a per species basis are allocated on an annual basis. You currently need to apply to Natural England for this (although government bodies and their agencies do have a habit of changing regularly) and for you to be granted a licence you will need to be able to demonstrate (with images) that you have the necessary experience of working at a nest site of a non-regulated species and be able to supply references from two other photographers who have previously held licences. At the end of the season you will be required to submit details of all the activity you have undertaken at your site. This might seem onerous, but I have heard it described as a privilege rather than a right to have the permissions necessary to work with these species and personally consider that to be the case. There is an unprecedented number of people involved in bird photography these days and at times the pressure on individual birds is all too obvious when you are at some sites, so ensuring a sound legal framework for the species under greatest pressure is highly appropriate.

Negative public perceptions of working at or near nests generally, along with a decline in demand from an editorial sales perspective, has meant that this area of photography is often shunned these days, which is a shame as, practised well and responsibly, images taken in this setting have a useful role to play in the promotion of conservation generally. Good practice, though, cannot be over-emphasized. The safe principles of working a hide into position as outlined earlier are even more imperative here. Put simply, if there is any sign of impacting on birds' behaviour, particularly when feeding the young, the project should be stopped. You really do need to do your research on the species you plan to work with – for instance, do both parents feed the young? If so, make sure you see both of them returning to the nest with food or you are impacting on the natural course of events. You should avoid visiting the hide, even if it is established, when the weather is extreme – hot or cold temperatures or heavy rain will make the feeding more difficult and the survival of the chicks generally more challenging, and disturbance should be minimized. Any so-called gardening that opens up the nest site for improved visibility for your images should be avoided; it makes the nest accessible to predators and the elements. Finally, keep the location as secret as possible – the fewer people who know about it, the less the level of disturbance. You may behave well during a short visit, but if there are constant short visits from others there will be no respite for the parents and young at all.

The bottom line with all of this is that you really shouldn't consider working at or near a nest site unless your knowledge, experience and understanding of the species is appropriate. Ask yourself the same challenging questions that you'd expect if you had to explain your working methods in person to the Schedule 1 panel; it's a good acid test. This is an area of photography where it really does pay to have spent some time with someone who has experience; the best way to learn is actually working well with that person.

You might also consider that most nesting birds will also have perches that they will naturally choose to sit on with beakfuls of food before they return to

▲ Fig. 8.16
This Meadow Pipit *Anthus pratensis*, a ground nester using a swathe of bracken for additional protection, would regularly sit on this frond before heading to the nest to feed its young. For the first couple of visits I made sure it headed straight from there to the nest to ensure I wasn't disturbing it by my presence.

feed their young. Although the same common sense and good practice is required, the perches are generally a distance away from the nest site itself and so offer just as interesting a photographic opportunity.

STALKING

This final aspect of fieldcraft is by and large based on common sense. There are many occasions when using any form of hide is both impossible and impractical and so working your way closer to a bird you've identified in a particular location is necessary. Firstly it is important to keep quiet and take your time in the approach. Keep low and use whatever cover there is available, positioning it between you and your subject to block your approach as best you can. You need to be as flexible as possible, so leave your backpack and anything you don't need behind when you begin the approach. It is also important to pre-visualize the image before you begin. Look at the position of the light and the background; it may be that you need to work round to a different angle to get a better position. Break your approach into stages; it's a good idea to get an 'in habitat' shot in the bag as you do this just in case you never get close enough and also to see if the shutter firing is likely to spook the bird. Finally, as with all fieldcraft activities, be prepared for a high failure rate. Most of the time you will find nothing or get no images at all, but every experience adds to your skill set and should improve your approach next time. When it does all come together you will get a great deal of satisfaction from it, especially knowing that you have gained the images in a responsible manner.

Chapter 9

Some Thoughts on Post-Capture Processing and Organization

In the days when film and slide dominated the photographic scene, which isn't all that long ago in real time but with the pace of change in the last ten years seems like an age ago, you either spent a great deal of money on your processing costs or dabbled in the chemical mysteries of the darkroom. For most people, the latter was just a bit of fun and probably restricted to a few monochrome reproductions since the criticality of the process and water temperatures along with the cost of kit required for colour printing was prohibitive for many.

The arrival of the digital age and the transfer of this post-capture process from a third party lab or your own garage to a computer in your home or a laptop out in the field even spawned years of debate as to what did or didn't constitute appropriate processing adjustments.

In reality both eras and their associated technologies were and are capable of their own malpractices, but there is little doubt that the digital age offers the greatest and easiest opportunities to make wholesale changes to an original image; with that come the inevitable differences of opinion as to what is right and what is not. Bird photography falls into one of the potentially most argumentative areas of all in this respect. Recording natural history and the artistic presentation of birdlife lead to very different interpretations of what is acceptable and what is not.

Suffice it to say that at the end of the day it up to individuals and ultimately their own conscience to choose what they want to do. From Camera Clubs to major international competitions, there are clear rules and guidelines as to what manipulation is or isn't allowed and it is up to photographers to adhere to them if they choose to enter their work. However, if your photography is purely for your own benefit and you enjoy the post-processing creativity as much as the in-camera approach, that is of course entirely your choice.

Throughout this book there has been a lot of emphasis on getting it as right as possible in camera, partly because it avoids contention but also from both a quality and practical perspective. Well-exposed and well-composed images need the least amount of work done to them, which means more time in the field photographing and enjoying nature; poorly exposed and composed images need more recovery time and it isn't always possible to do this work without a massive decrease in quality of the final file.

What follows in this chapter is therefore not a catch-all for photo processing or image recovery, rather a reflection on how to get sensibly organized and how to make sure you understand some simple steps that will routinely squeeze a little more out of even a well-composed and well-exposed image – something that every file will benefit from.

◀ Fig. 9.1
Hawfinch *Coccothraustes coccothruastes* at the edge of a pool, Netherlands. Canon 1D Mk4, ƒ5.6, 1/1600sec, ISO 200.

ESTABLISHING
A WORKFLOW

The more images you take, the more folders and files you will generate, and over time it will become increasingly hard to remember what is where on your hard drive(s). It's important therefore to establish a simple and logical workflow to managing your images as you transfer them from your camera into the processing and archiving arena.

This is in essence nothing more complex than good file management. A useful place to start is to name a new folder using a description easily interpreted several months or years later, such as a location or subject, month and year (Skomer June 2012, for example). Within this, creating a sub-folder called RAW files into which all the RAWs from the camera can be transferred, either by plugging the camera into your computer or using a card reader, is a logical next step. If you treat this sub-folder a little like the wallet of negatives you used to have in the days of film, it ensures that you will always have an original place to go back to to find your image

original. Batch re-naming all of these RAW files using the folder name is another way of making this process of backtracking even easier, and most image software will allow this very easily.

PROCESSING RAW FILES

When it comes to processing your images there is an array of different software options. If you have decided that the simpler approach of JPEGs is the easiest for you then many of the simple modifications, which are described below, are achievable using the software that would have come with your camera or free downloadable programs such as Google's Picasa. JPEG processing does have its limitations, though, as certain aspects such as white balance are not able to be modified at all. In quality terms, the TIFF or JPEG you output from your RAW file will be of the highest order – the same as straight out of the camera in fact, as processing applied to a RAW file is totally non-destructive, unlike that to a

▶ Fig. 9.2
Creating logically named and dated folders for your images based on a principle such as 'where and when' will make the finding of material at a later date a lot easier and faster.

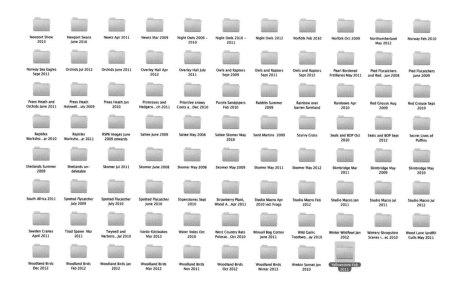

▲ Fig. 9.3
This image of a Yellow Wagtail *Motacilla flava* will benefit from a slight crop to improve composition. This will reduce the file size by around 10%. Start to go too much more than that, especially when the reason is to make the subject bigger, and the end quality will begin to suffer.

JPEG. RAW processing is possible with the software provided with your camera, and most programs such as Photoshop CS, or it's cheaper and smaller cousin Photoshop Elements, will not only do this but also supply all the further image management, layout and printing you may require.

With further specialist RAW software packages such as Capture One and Lightroom also available, there is plenty of choice and also plenty of room for confusion. It is generally best to start with something basic like Photoshop Elements and then progress once you have the experience and confidence to do so. Read reviews, talk to other photographers and download trial versions before making any final decisions. The images used to cover the simple recommended image management steps that follow are from the interface of Capture One, but the headings and principles will apply to all software in this arena.

Cropping

Although it is always best to compose your images in camera (as has been covered already in this book), there will always be times when some cropping is required – the removal of a distracting element or the need for a slight re-positioning of the subject in the final framing, for instance. The crop tool will allow you to work on either a freehand basis or lock in a certain ratio. Given that most SLRs take images in a 3:2 ratio in the first place, it makes sense to try working on a similar basis if possible. Other ratios (square or panoramic) can also work well on some images as well.

Closely aligned to the crop tool is the rotation tool, which allows you to rotate the image to level out any horizons or water levels that aren't perfectly straight. It will slightly crop the image in the process, so look carefully as you go to check that this isn't removing an important element of the composition.

▲ Fig. 9.4
Because I was lying flat to the floor when photographing this Coot
Fulica atra I ended up getting a slightly angled horizon. A simple
rotation will straighten this up, though.

▲ Fig. 9.5
The two circles you can see on this in-process image of a Redshank
Tringa totanus show where it has been necessary to use the dust
spot remover tool; because the background areas are reasonably
uniform it will be fine to do this at the RAW conversion stage.

Cleaning Dust Spots

It's actually only reasonably recently that the cleaning of dust spots – either those that have been attracted to the sensor or because you haven't kept the glass elements on the front or rear of your lens very clean – has actually become possible. It used to be necessary to use either the so-called Clone stamp or Healing brush in Photoshop. Many dust spots are easier to remove in this post-RAW processing stage, especially if they are in areas of complex colour and texture change; if they occur on a clean background or single colour then getting rid of them at this stage using the RAW converter's own tools is easiest.

Contrast (Shadows and Highlights)

This is probably the most critical area of the RAW conversion process as contrast is what will re-introduce punch and impact into your images. Back in Chapter 2 the topic of the histogram was covered in some detail. When you look at your image on-screen in your RAW conversion software, the reason for looking to control it at point of capture becomes even more clear as it is the re-positioning of the black point and the white point on the image's histogram that will re-establish this contrast. Depending on your specific software and starting with the black point, this can be achieved by grabbing the pointer on the far left of the histogram (which represents pure black in the image) and sliding it to the left to a position just outside the data in the image's histogram. In some programs this is achieved by means of a slider rather than grabbing the point itself, but the principle is the same. You will see the darker parts (or shadows) of your image get darker while you are doing this. The next

stage is to do the reverse with the white point at the extreme right, again pulling it into a position just outside the main histogram. Take great care here not to go too far, as you want to avoid clipping the image and losing detail in the whites. Finally you can impact the general mood or brightness of the image by sliding the midpoint to the histogram – to the right and you lighten the mid-tones and feel of the image, to the left and you darken it. The first two stages are standard practice, but the final step here is very judgemental. Each image will require a different approach based on how you want to portray it and how you remember the scene.

At this stage you can also consider whether to apply a further small amount of saturation to the image if you feel that this contrast-enhancing step hasn't quite done enough for your liking. For this you can use the straightforward saturation slider, which acts just like the controls on your television, applying a boost to all the colours. Or, depending on which software you are using, the vibrance or clarity sliders will apply the boost only to the less saturated parts of the image, which is more subtle in its approach.

As with everything to do with post-processing, take great care not to overdo it. Nothing looks worse than an over-saturated and unnatural image; all your good work in the field can be lost in an instant of over-zealousness at the computer. Too much boosting here can also introduce unwanted amounts of digital noise, which is also to be avoided.

▲ Fig. 9.6
This image of a Black-winged Stilt *Himantopus himantopus* has, like
all images, benefitted from some additional contrast achieved by
moving the black and white points on the histogram (or levels) on
the left of the screen. The mid-point has also been slightly darkened
to increase the intensity of the early morning light.

▲ Fig. 9.7
The same image has now had a small amount of saturation applied
to it to further help and is now ready for conversion to a TIFF.

Sharpening

There are filters on the sensor of your SLR that are designed to reduce the amount of unwanted digital noise and unusual artefacts or patterns on your images. One of the side-effects of these is that RAW files in particular will often look a little soft, or rather lacking in crispness around the defined edges of clear objects. You can apply in-camera sharpening to all your images, but it is best to leave the camera set to neutral in this respect and apply the sharpening as you process your RAW file. Again, it is important not to overdo it; your RAW conversion software will have a standard default based on the camera and lens combination that was used to take the image. This is generally a pretty good starting point and needs little change most of the time, but as a final element of your RAW processing you should check to see that it is acceptable. As with saturation, avoid over-sharpening as it can once again introduce digital noise, and a seriously over-sharpened image can start to look very pixellated and generally messy.

Converting for Output

Once you have made all the simple, required adjustments to your image it is time to output a version in whatever file format you choose. File formats have been discussed in previous chapters, but at this stage and for any general further editing in Photoshop then the maximum quality format that comes from a TIFF file is recommended. Set your size at 300 pixels per inch, as this is the resolution most used in all aspects of the industry (image libraries, magazines, etc.) and is also perfect for any printing that you may look to do with the images yourself. You also need to set the colour space of the image and for the general purposes described above Adobe RGB is recommended.

There are a number of additional advantages to working with RAW files that become apparent at this outputting stage. The sizing and specification just described is ideal for the vast majority of general image needs and will maintain maximum file size and quality through to the end of the process. If, however, you want to put an image onto a website, say, then a huge TIFF will be too big, and on the internet the full range of colours associated with the Adobe RGB colour space will not be visible. Instead you can set the image size to 72 dpi, adjust the colour space to SRGB and output the file as a JPEG (maybe even one that you have pre-determined the exact size of – 600 pixels on the longest side, for instance), and you will be presented with an identical image to the TIFF but in a size and colour space ready to email or add to your website, Flickr album or Facebook page.

Keywording and Archiving

The final stage of managing your files is to make sure that you have done everything you can to find them again and ensure that they are safely stored and backed up.

The first stage of this is to organize all the files that you have output from your RAW conversions. You can either leave them within the master folder where you have kept your RAW files, or it might make sense to start to build folders of either different types of wildlife (birds, insects, mammals, etc.) if your photography is of a more general nature or if you are a pure bird photographer maybe go one stage down in terms of classification and look at folders for waders, seabirds, birds of prey, passerines etc.

Within these folders you should then simply add the bird name to the date and location labelling that you applied when batch-inputting your RAW files. What this will do is allow you to easily find your way back to the original RAW if necessary and also by adding the species name you will be able to search the folder for all your images of that species.

The next stage is to add keywords to the image to further facilitate searching. If you are supplying images to an image library or any other end user, providing fuller information about the image will prove of use to them and the search engines their online websites might also use. Keywords are metadata that remain embedded in the image wherever it goes, so it also makes sense to include some copyright and contact details relating to yourself in there as well. Some RAW converters allow you to add keywords before the outputting stage; it can equally easily be done using Adobe Bridge, which is the file management system that comes with Photoshop, and the illustrations used here are from within that software.

Storage and Back-up

The final stage is to make sure that both your master folders of RAW files and the multiple folders of key-worded TIFFs and JPEGs you have created from them are safely stored. Until you have suffered the pain that goes with a hard drive failure you might not consider it essential, but having more than one copy of all of your folders is really essential and good practice – cameras and lenses, expensive as they are, can be replaced, but lost images can't.

Files and folders are too big to consider CDs and DVDs as anything other than temporary or portable storage these days, so using external hard drives is the way to go. Quality is now generally good and they can be purchased in units of terabytes now and at very affordable prices. For increased security, stacked suites of hard drives in units from manufacturers such as Drobo provide additional security. They multi-store your folders across all the hard drives in them so that if even two drives fail at once they are still backed up. You could also consider the option of having one of your back-ups stored away from home – a safety deposit box or a relative's house, for instance, in case the worst should happen to your home.

▲ Fig. 9.8
Using Adobe Bridge it is quite easy to add keywords by simply ticking the box of those you have created already in your menu system to add to a new image. If you need a new one you simply create it using 'Add Keyword'.

▲ Fig. 9.9
Freestanding hard drive units such as this are flexible and economic ways of ensuring all your images and RAW files are backed up safely.

Appendix

RPS GUIDELINES FOR NATURE PHOTOGRAPHY

The Nature Group of the Royal Photographic Society produced a set of guidelines for photographers back in the 1960s. These were revised in both 1997 and 2007 in consultation with the RSPB and the three statutory Nature Conservation Councils. It seems appropriate to include them in full as an appendix to this work for the purposes of clarity and also to highlight the specific legislation that applies in certain areas (some of it to other elements of nature photography as well as birds).

There is one hard and fast rule, whose spirit must be observed at all times: *'The welfare of the subject is more important than the photograph.'*

Introduction

Photography should not be undertaken if it puts the subject at risk. Risk to the subject, in this context, means risk of disturbance, physical damage, causing anxiety, consequential predation, and lessened reproductive success.

Photography may be seen as a criminal offence with relation to some species, since disturbance will be occasioned. Many species are afforded special legal protection. The Law as it affects nature photography must be observed. For Great Britain the main legislation is listed at the end of this leaflet. In other countries one should find out in advance any restrictions that apply.

Apparent lax or absence of local legislation should not lead any photographer to relax his/her own high standard.

General

The photographer should be familiar with the natural history of the subject; the more complex the life-form and the rarer the species, the greater his/her knowledge must be. He/she should also be sufficiently familiar with other natural history subjects to be able to avoid damaging their interests accidentally. Photography of uncommon creatures and plants by people who know nothing of the hazards to species and habitat is to be deplored.

With reference to Sites of Special Scientific Interest (SSSIs): anyone who intentionally or recklessly destroys or damages any of the flora, fauna, geological or physio-graphical features by reason of which a site is of special interest, or intentionally or recklessly disturbs any of those fauna, is guilty of an offence and is liable on summary conviction to a fine.

It is important for the good name of nature photography that its practitioners observe normal

▲ I'm not normally a fan of busy backgrounds, but the vibrancy of the berries along with the fact they matched this male Blackbird's (*Turdus merula*) beak in colour along with the combination of sharp as well as out of focus berries makes the setting work.

▲ When looking to capture portrait images sometimes bold and tight compositions work well such as this Common Crane *Grus grus*.

▲ Crested Tits *Lophophanes cristatus* are among the flightiest birds to photograph, so when working with them at a feeding station it often pays to pre-visualise a composition and set up for it in anticipation of the bird arriving in place next time it visits.

social courtesies. Permission should be obtained before working on private land and other naturalists should not be incommoded. Work at sites and colonies which are subjects of special study should be coordinated with the people concerned.

Photographs of dead, stuffed, homebred, captive, cultivated, or otherwise controlled specimens may be of genuine value but should never be passed off as wild and free. Users of such photographs (irrespective of the purpose for which it is thought they will be used) should always be informed, regardless of how little they may seem to care.

Birds at the Nest

The terms of the Wildlife and Countryside Act 1981 must be complied with at all times. It is an offence to recklessly or intentionally disturb a Schedule 1 species while it is building a nest, or is in, on or near a nest containing eggs or young; or to disturb the dependant young of such a species. In Scotland it is an offence to recklessly or intentionally disturb or harass any Schedule 1A bird (i.e. White-tailed Eagle) or any Schedule 1 bird which leks (i.e. Capercaillie). A licence is necessary to photograph Schedule 1 birds in certain circumstances. Licences can be obtained from the appropriate Statutory Nature Conservation body.

Photography of birds at the nest should only be undertaken by those with a good knowledge of bird breeding behaviour. There are many competent photographers (and bird-watchers) who lack this qualification. Scarce species should only be photographed in an area where they may be relatively frequent; it is therefore preferable to photograph British rarities overseas where they may be commoner. Photographers working abroad should exercise the same care as they would at home. A hide should always be used if there is a reasonable doubt that birds would continue normal breeding behaviour otherwise. No part of the occupant should be visible from the outside of the hide. Hides should not be erected where the attention of the public or a predator is likely to be attracted. If there is any such risk, an assistant should be in the vicinity to keep potential intruders away. No hide should be left unattended in daylight in a place with common public access.

▲ Looking ahead was key to this shot of a pair of Eider *Somateria mollisima* photographed in Iceland– having seen the contrast offered by the hole in the iceberg when the female swam by it was a question of watching for the male to follow into position as he followed her.

Visits to a site should be kept to a minimum to avoid damage to vegetation and the creation of new tracks or pathways. The site should be restored to natural-ness between sessions. Reported nest failures due to nest photography are few, but a high proportion of those that occur are due to undue haste. The maximum possible time should elapse between stages of hide movement or erection, introduction of lens or flash equipment, gardening and occupation. Many species need preparation at least a week in advance; this should be seen as the norm. Each stage should be fully accepted by the bird (or birds, where feeding or incubation is shared) before the next stage is initi-ated. If a stage is refused by the birds (which should be evident from their behaviour to a competent bird

photographer) the procedure should be reversed at least one stage; if refusal is repeated photography should be abandoned. The period of disturbance caused by each stage should be kept to a minimum. It is undesirable to initiate a stage in late evening, when the birds' activities are becoming less frequent. Remote-control work where acceptance cannot be checked is rarely satisfactory. Resetting of a shutter or manually advancing film is even less likely to be acceptable because of the frequency of disturbance. While the best photographs are often obtained about the time of hatching this is not the time to start erecting a hide – nor when eggs are fresh. It is better to wait until the reactions of the parent birds to the situation are firmly established.

▲ Having watched this Kingfisher *Alcedo atthis* dive off this bull rush on several occasions I thought I had established a movement that he seemed to make pre-dive. Although several failed attempts challenged my theory eventually I caught the precise positioning that I was after.

▲ Working at the nest with any bird such as this Lesser Spotted Woodpecker *Dendrocopos minor* requires a great deal of judgment and observation to ensure that you are not disturbing them and reducing the frequency with which they return to feed their young. It pays to watch from a distance before photographing to get a feel for this in advance and then again from a distance having finished to ensure all continues normally so you can judge whether returning the next day is sensible or not.

The birds' first visits to the nest after the hide is occupied are best used for checking routes and behaviour rather than for exposures. The quieter the shutter, the less the chance of birds objecting to it. The longer the focal length of the lens used, the more distant the hide can be and the less risk of the birds not accepting it. Nesting birds photographed from a hide can be put under pressure if too many photographers are waiting for 'their turn' in the hide. Each change of photographer causes fresh disturbance and should be avoided. Ideally two photographers working together should be the norm – two to enter the hide and one to leave, although more may be required for some species. Disturbance should always be kept to an absolute minimum and should never be caused during bad weather (rain or exceptionally hot sun). The trapping of breeding birds for studio-type photography is totally unacceptable in any circumstances and an offence3 under the WCA.

It is an offence to remove nestlings or eggs from the nest for photography even on a temporary basis; when photographed in situ care should be taken not to cause an 'explosion' of young from the nest.

▲ Bold compositions like these Atlantic Puffin *Fratercula arctica*, which rely on lots of space to tell the story, offer good usage potential for designers if selling your work is a factor in your shooting.

It is never permissible to artificially restrict the free movement of the young.

The use of playback tape or stuffed predators (to stimulate territorial or alarm reactions) should not be undertaken near the nest in the breeding season. Additionally the use of bait or song tapes to attract birds to the camera, even though this is away from the nest, should not be undertaken in an occupied breeding territory. Use of such methods may be considered illegal with respect to Schedule 1 species.

Mammals and Birds Away from the Nest

Predators should not be baited from a hide in an area where hides may later be used for photography of birds at the nest. Wait and see photography should not be undertaken in an area where a hide may show irresponsible shooters and trappers that targets exist; this is particularly important overseas. The capture of even non-breeding birds for photography under controlled conditions is not an acceptable or legal practice. Incidental photography of birds taken under licence for some valid scientific purpose is acceptable provided it causes minimal delay to the

▲ Photographing white birds on white backgrounds such as this winter
plumage Ptarmigan *Lagopus mutus* in the Cairngorms, is a test of
your camera and your processing skills. Over exposing by 2 stops to
make sure the whites are truly white (even a marginal over exposure
is preferable) and then returning some contrast with a simple Levels
or Curves adjustment to the RAW file is generally the best approach.

bird's release. If any extra delay is involved it would
need to be covered by the terms of the licence.
Taking small mammals for photographic purposes
is not recommended. In exceptional cases where
captivity is necessary it should only be carried out
provided they are not breeding (either sex) and are
released with minimum delay in their original habitat. No attempt should be made to tame any animal
so taken as it jeopardizes their survival. Hibernating
animals should never be awakened for photography.

Specially Protected Animals

Threatened species such as Otters, Red Squirrels and
Dormice are given full protection under Schedule 5
of the Wildlife and Countryside Act. The restrictions
on photographing these species at their places of
shelter are exactly the same as those for nesting
birds. Not all protected species have regular places of
shelter; these include two reptiles, two amphibians
and several very rare butterflies and moths. The best
rule is, 'if in doubt, don't'. For example do not move
objects in the habitat in search of smooth snakes
to photograph. Bats need special care. Disturbance
at or near a breeding colony of any bat may cause
desertion of an otherwise safe site; all bats are

◀ On a long lens such as a 500mm or more the depth of field is exaggeratedly small so when photographing 2 birds such as this Red-Throated Diver *Gavia stellata* and her young, it needs patience and careful observation to wait until they are in exactly the same narrow band of focus.

▲ Photographing this Shag *Phalocrocorax aristotelis* in heavy falling snow it was necessary to switch to manual focusing in order to fix on the bird accurately – large snowflakes can through your autofocus system off and leave it either constantly hunting or focused on a snowflake in front of the bird.

▲ This image of a bathing Starling *Sturnus vulgaris* photographed in Hungary is made all the more dramatic by the backlighting on the water droplets he is creating as he splashes. This shot was only possible here in the afternoon when the sun was in the right place.

▶ This image of a White-tailed Eagle *Haliaeetus albicilla* catching a fish was deliberately underexposed to ensure that the background went dark and provided the maximum contrast with the sunlit bird, thereby increasing the drama of the shot.

▶ Normally I would recommend position a bird flying into frame closer to the line of thirds than this Brown Pelican *Pelicanus occidentalis* has ended up, but the splash of water behind him as he takes off ensures the image remains balanced.

specially protected and none may be disturbed or photographed in a roost except with a licence from the appropriate Statutory Nature Conservation body. Bats are acutely sensitive to disturbance. There is evidence that important hibernation sites have been permanently deserted as a result of disturbance caused by photography. Licences to photograph are normally issued only to experienced bat workers. No fully protected species may be taken from the wild without a licence, and taking means any form of capture including the use of butterfly nets. Some further animals, included on Schedule 6 of the Act, are protected from trapping, and these include shrews, hedgehogs and pine martens. If you need to trap these species in order to photograph them you must apply for a licence. Disturbance of any European protected species anywhere is an offence under the Habitat Regulations 1994.

▲ Careful hiding of some fat on the rear of this lichen covered branch proved a necessary attraction for these Long-Tailed Tits *Aegithalos caudatus* to visit. I had set up my camera in perfect parallel to the branch to increase the chances of getting both birds in focus.

▲ Once you move beyond simply capturing what's in front of you with your camera then looking to get the personality of your subject across becomes more important: the nosy and inquisitive nature of this Shag *Phalocrocorax aristotelis* is best achieved in this head on approach, with careful focusing on the eyes requiring use of a single focal point to achieve.

Other Animals

For cold-blooded animals and invertebrates, temporary removal from the wild to a studio or vivarium (or aquarium) for photography is not recommended; where practicable field photographs are to be preferred. If a subject is removed from the wild for photography it should be released as soon as possible in its original habitat.

It is illegal to take from the wild, species listed on Schedule 5 of the Wildlife and Countryside Act, or take by means such as live-traps, species on Schedule 6. Insect photographers should be familiar with those species, which may not be taken without a licence. Chilling or anaesthesia for quietening invertebrates should not be undertaken.

▷ Identification rings such as these very pronounced ones on this Egyptian Vulture *Nephron percnopterus* photographed in Bulgaria, are the bain of many photographers lives. I tend to avoid cloning them out and rather concentrate on non-ringed subjects instead, but in this instance they helped with the identification of this particular bird – almost 30 years old at the time of shooting this image and a regular returner to the area to breed each year she was also onto her second mate already too!

▷ Spending time with common and accessible birds such as this winter plumage Black Headed Gull *Chroicocephalus ridibundus* on a north Norfolk beach is a good way to learn the skill of watching a birds behaviour and the ability to predict when it will do something interesting, in this case give out a typically raucous call

When microhabitats (e.g. tree-bark, beach rocks, etc.) have been disturbed, they should be restored after the photography. There should be no damage to habitat; any that does occur may be illegal on nature reserves, or SSSIs, even if the landowner has given permission.

Plants

Photographers should be clear about existing legislation. It is an offence[3] to uproot any wild plant without the permission of the landowner or his tenant. For over a hundred very threatened plants, including the rarest orchids, the law extends to picking, so any damage to surrounding vegetation, which may include young plants, must be avoided. If photography comes to be seen as a threat, rather

▲ The affection that this pair of Gannets *Morus bassanus* has for one another may be a human emotion applied to birds, but such interactions are part of making the whole process of watching and photographing birds as engaging a pastime as it is, and generally gets a reaction from even non-interested parties!

than an aid, to rare plant conservation, pressures may mount for more restrictive legislation such as giving protected plants at flowering time similar protection to that enjoyed by Schedule 1 birds at nesting time.

No rarity should ever be picked (still less dug up) for studio photography, or to facilitate the in situ photography of another specimen. Nor should any part of one be removed to facilitate the photography of another plant.

For some subjects (botanical/fungi/etc.) some 'gardening' (i.e. tidying up of the surrounding vegetation) may be necessary. This should be kept to a minimum to avoid exposing the subject to predators, people, or weather. Plants or branches should be tied back rather than cut off and the site restored to as natural a condition as possible after any photographic session. The aim should always be to leave no obvious signs of disturbance. If an image of a rarity is to be published or exhibited, care should be taken that the site location is not accidentally given away. Take care that your photograph does not contain any clues as to the whereabouts of the specimen; this is particularly important in wide-angle photographs. Sites of rarities should never deliberately be disclosed except for conservation purposes.

Fungi

Other than a few very common species, it is rarely possible to identify fungi either in situ or from a photograph; a photograph of an unidentified or incorrectly identified species is of very limited value. Therefore it is usually necessary to collect a specimen after photographing them. This should be done with a knife rather than the fingers, taking care to collect the entire specimen including any base, which may be immersed in the substrate. Notes should be made of the substrate (in particular for mycorrhizal genera) and any associated organisms, as this may aid identification. One of the first principles of collecting is to leave the environment as close as possible to the state in which it was found. Any logs that are rolled over should be returned to their original position. If working as a group, then only the most experienced mycologist should collect specimens as his analysis can later be communicated to the other photographers. He/she may need to collect five or six specimens of differing ages to enable a mycologist to make an accurate identification after microscopic analysis, and also have sufficient specimens left over to store in a herbarium for future reference. It may not be necessary to collect the entire specimen in the case of very large species, i.e. brackets, as a wedge taken from the side is often sufficient. Be aware that some public open spaces are subject to local byelaws that may prohibit collecting. Four species are legally protected from collection anywhere in England, Scotland and Wales, even for scientific purposes, by Schedule 8 of the Wildlife and Countryside Act 1981 (species covered are *Hericium erinaceus*, *Piptoporus quercinus*, *Boletus regius* and *Battarrea phalloides*).

The Truth of the Final Image

A nature photograph should convey the essential truth of what the photographer saw at the time it was taken.

No radical changes should be made to the original photograph, nor additions made from any source, whether during processing in the darkroom, or through digital/electronic manipulation. The removal of minor blemishes or distractions is permissible.

Legislation and Schedules

The photographer should be aware of the appropriate sections of the following, and any subsequent 'amendments':

- The Wildlife and Countryside Act 1981
- The Wildlife (Northern Ireland) Order 1985
- Protection of Badgers Act 1992
- The Butterfly Society Conservation Code
- Botanical Society of the British Isles (BSBI) list of rare plants and Code of Conduct
- The RSPB leaflet 'Bird Photography and the Law'
- The Conservation (Natural Habitats, etc.) Regulations 1994
- The Countryside & Rights of Way Act 2000
- Natural Environment & Rural Communities Act 2006

These guidelines are reproduced by kind permission of the Royal Photographic Society (www.rps.org).